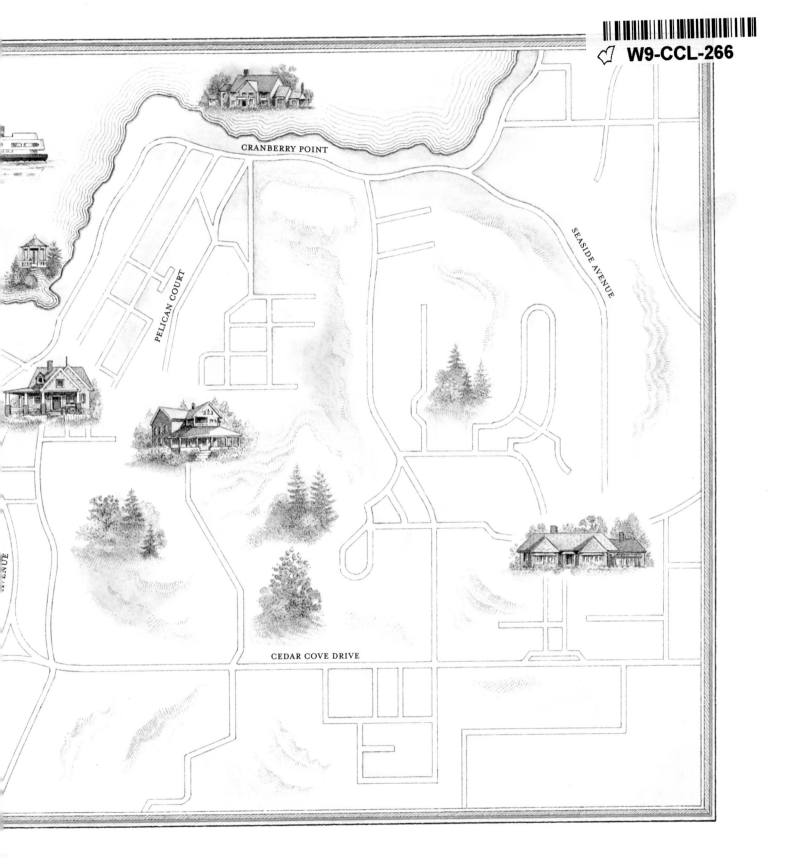

CRANBERRY POINT

PELICAN COURT

SEASIDE AVENUE

CEDAR COVE DRIVE

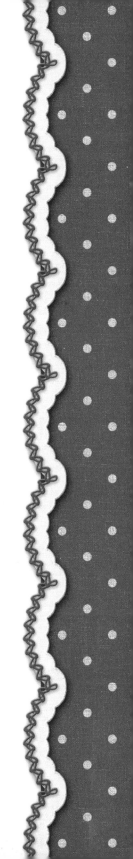

DEBBIE MACOMBER'S
CEDAR COVE COOKBOOK

Photographs by

ANDY RYAN

Illustrations by

DEBORAH CHABRIAN

HARLEQUIN®

OTHER CEDAR COVE BOOKS BY DEBBIE MACOMBER

92 Pacific Boulevard • 8 Sandpiper Way • 74 Seaside Avenue

6 Rainier Drive • 50 Harbor Street • 44 Cranberry Point • 311 Pelican Court

204 Rosewood Lane • 16 Lighthouse Road

HARLEQUIN®

Debbie Macomber's Cedar Cove Cookbook

ISBN-13: 978-0373-89213-6
ISBN-10: 0-373-89213-6

Library of Congress Cataloging-in-Publication Data

Macomber, Debbie.
[Cedar Cove Cookbook]
Debbie Macomber's Cedar Cove Cookbook.
p. cm.
Includes index.
ISBN 978-0-373-89213-6 (hardcover)
1. Cookery. 2. Cedar Cove (Wash. : Imaginary place) I. Title. II. Title: Cedar Cove Cookbook.
TX714.M332 2009
641.5—dc22   2008053711

www.eHarlequin.com

Printed in U.S.A.

Book Design: Susi Oberhelman
Photography: Andy Ryan
Food Stylist: Catrine Kelty
Prop Stylist: Sylvia Lachter
Recipe Developer: Susan Lilly Ott
Fabric illustrations: Karen Stimson, www.woolsweaterstreet.com

Contents

Appetizers 78

at 311 Pelican Court with
Zach and Rosie Cox

Dinner 94

at 44 Cranberry Point
with Bob and Peggy Beldon

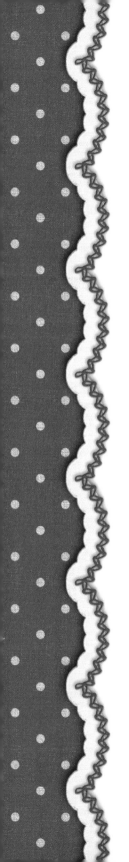

Introduction

As I've often said, I'm a frequent eater—but I'm a frequent cook, too! In fact, I spend more time in the kitchen than I do in the dining room. I remember, when I was only four, begging my mother to let me help her make dinner. She was a gifted cook who never let a recipe get in the way of being creative; not surprisingly, working in the kitchen (and enjoying it!) is part of my family heritage.

I think it's fair to say that, thanks to my mother, I became proficient at cooking over the years. Good thing, too—in high school, the cooking part of Home Economics was all that got me a passing grade. I'm a terrible seamstress, so my ability to cook saved me from a certain F. (Who knew there were so many incorrect ways to sew in a zipper?)

In the days before the many cookbooks now available—cookbooks for every conceivable type of cuisine and diet and specialty—recipes were often preserved on index cards. My mom had several small green boxes stuffed with them. And after her death I found a notebook in which my grandmother had written down recipes and cooking hints she felt her daughter (my mom) should have when she left home. I savored every word and learned cooking hints I still use. For instance, I discovered how to gauge when bean soup has simmered long enough to reach its maximum flavor. According to my grandma, Helen Zimmerman, you can tell by the aroma. As a thrifty and inventive cook, she also had lots of suggestions for substitutes and alternative ingredients, and different spices to try in particular recipes.

Like my mother, I've collected recipes all my life—and yes, I have the same small green recipe boxes crammed with carefully handwritten notes that date back to my grade-school days.

Years ago, I chose some of those recipes and created my own envelope-size recipe booklets as a thank-you gift to my loyal readers at Christmas. In return,

readers sent me their own favorite recipes. This was my first venture into cookbook publishing—but not my last!

You may have noticed that meals play an important role in all my stories. This is certainly true of earlier series like "Midnight Sons" and "Heart of Texas," as well as the Blossom Street books. But cooking and preparing meals, and sharing them with family and friends, is perhaps most significant in my Cedar Cove series.

If you've read any of these stories, you'll recognize Charlotte Jefferson Rhodes. She's known and loved by just about everyone in town. Not only that, her reputation as a superlative cook is well-deserved.

In this book, Charlotte's going to take you on a tour of the kitchens and dining rooms of Cedar Cove. She'll share her best recipes, including those she was given by members of her family and her many friends. She's also going to fill you in on what's been happening with the people in town—her daughter, Olivia Griffin, her granddaughter, Justine Gunderson, Zach and Rosie Cox and Grace Harding, to name a few.

Like Charlotte, I believe that food is central to the important relationships in our lives. Serving a meal is probably the ultimate expression of hospitality and friendship, and a good dinner sustains us in more than just the obvious ways. For me, for Charlotte—and, in fact, for most of us—the preparation of food is associated with enjoyment, comfort, *love*.

While sharing food is a social activity, sharing recipes can bind us with others, too—with friends and perhaps especially with our families. It's about forming and nurturing traditions, which help us create a sense of continuity from one generation to the next.

Quite a few of the recipes I use today came from my mother and grandmother—recipes I've passed on to my own children. Just as some of Charlotte's recipes come from her mother and were passed down to her daughter, Olivia, and now her granddaughter, Justine....

Justine, who's opened a tea room in town, has asked Charlotte for recipes and menu ideas, hoping to make her restaurant as wonderful as a visit to the fragrant kitchen she remembers from her grandmother's home. Happy to comply, Charlotte has collected her favorite recipes in this book. You might recognize some of them from scenes in the Cedar Cove stories.

Ultimately, the genesis of this cookbook is my readers' requests for these very recipes, the ones I've mentioned in the novels. My goal is always to give you a satisfying reading experience—with something extra. I like to describe myself as a "value-added" author, and this cookbook is one way of offering you that extra value. So are Charlotte's introductions, in which she reveals her insights about the people of Cedar Cove, and her personal comments on various recipes.

Please join Charlotte and everyone in town for lots of delightful adventures in cooking and dozens of memorable meals. I hope these recipes will be as treasured in your family as they are in Charlotte's (and in mine).

It's a privilege to share my own "kitchen heritage" with you—a heritage of good food and good times.

Happy reading…and happy eating!

Debbie Macomber

Breakfast

at **16 LIGHTHOUSE ROAD** with

Olivia Griffin

I should begin by introducing myself in case we haven't met before. I'm Charlotte Jefferson Rhodes and I've lived in Cedar Cove for much of my life. My beloved first husband, Clyde Jefferson (may he rest in peace), has been gone about twenty years now. We had two children—Will, our oldest, and Olivia Griffin (formerly Lockhart). Olivia lives in Cedar Cove and Will, now retired and divorced, recently moved back here. I remarried a few years ago, and Ben and I are very happy. There you have it—my personal history in one short paragraph.

I'm going to take you around Cedar Cove and share recipes I've accumulated over a lifetime—recipes I've discovered or created and many that have been passed to me by family and friends.

My daughter, Olivia, is a big believer in the value of a nutritious breakfast, so I think it's appropriate to start our journey of food and cooking at her house.

I've noticed, and I'm sure you have, too, that children develop their own personalities very early in life. Even at the

age of two, Olivia was an organized little girl. One day I found her in my closet straightening my shoes. At *two!* That same year at Christmas, she took charge of clearing away the wrapping paper.

From the time she was three or four, Olivia decided she wanted to help me in the kitchen. I let her, although she couldn't bear to crack an egg—for fear of dirtying her hands. She never licked a beater or a spoon, either. Several of the recipes I've included here are favorites of hers from childhood. Dishes she made herself from a young age.

By the age of five, when Olivia started school, she could already read and do simple math. Clyde was convinced she'd grow up to become an engineer. Back then, there were few women in such professions and as her mother I dreamed lofty dreams for my daughter. But I never would've guessed she'd become a family court judge!

In high school Olivia and her best friend, Grace, used to hang out at the Pancake Palace (established, as the sign proudly says, in 1950). In fact, the girls still meet there at least once a week. I replicated the Palace's pancake recipe for Olivia because she liked it so much, and I included it here.

Shortly after they graduated from high school, Grace married Dan Sherman, while Olivia went on to college, where she met Stanley Lockhart. I will say one thing, and only one thing, about my daughter's ex-husband. Stan turned out to be a bitter disappointment—to Olivia, to the kids and to me. Enough said. I may not have a high opinion of Stan but he is, after all, the father of my grandchildren. The Sour Cream Coffee Cake you'll find in these pages was one of his favorites, and it makes a nice addition to Sunday brunch.

Soon after her marriage, my daughter had twins, Jordan and Justine, followed by younger brother James. Olivia had set her sights on obtaining a law degree and with her usual sense of purpose she pursued this, all the while juggling family responsibilities and numerous other commitments. Thinking back on those early years I stand in awe of her. I can hardly believe how much she accomplished—and how effortless she made it look.

A few years later, Olivia was practicing law in Cedar Cove, and Stan was working in Seattle, taking the ferry into the city every morning and coming home at eight or nine in the evening. Efficient as ever, Olivia managed to keep the household running smoothly and still do well at her career. Then in August of 1986 our world was turned upside down. On a bright summer's day, Jordan and Justine went to the lake. Jordan dove into the water, broke his neck and drowned.

Olivia rarely mentions Jordan, although I know he's always in her thoughts. The death of a child forever scars a mother's heart. A grandmother's, too.

I was desperately worried about Olivia the year after Jordan's death. At the same time, Stanley chose to announce that he wanted out of the marriage and quickly filed for divorce. As you can imagine, Justine and James both faltered under the weight of these losses. But even then Olivia held the family together. Thankfully, Grace was there for her. During that horrible year Grace was the one constant in Olivia's life. I'd always liked her but that's when she won my unflagging love.

Despite the tragedy my daughter experienced, let me reassure you that Olivia's story is by no means depressing. She became a judge when Justine was still in high school. I like to stop by the courthouse now and then to watch her in action. (Frankly, I get some of my best knitting done there!)

A real turning point in Olivia's life came when she met Jack Griffin almost ten years ago. If ever two people were polar opposites it would be Olivia and Jack. He's the editor of *The Cedar Cove Chronicle* and about as disorganized as any man I know. The word *slob* must've been invented for him. He fell in love with Olivia so fast I still shake my head in wonder. I was delighted by their marriage, although it got off to a rocky start. Can you imagine my methodical, organized Olivia married to Jack? Still, their love is strong enough to allow them to compromise and they've figured out routines that work for both of them. Like eating a healthy breakfast. Jack used to grab a coffee and a couple of doughnuts on his way to work and call it breakfast. Olivia's finally persuaded him to have some granola or her Good Morning Strawberry-Banana Smoothie instead.

Remember Olivia's little saying: The better your breakfast, the better your day!

Good Morning Strawberry-Banana Smoothie

Serves 1

1 banana, cut into chunks and frozen at least 15 minutes

1 cup frozen strawberries, blueberries or raspberries

¼ cup orange juice

1 6-ounce container (¾ cup) nonfat plain yogurt

Creamy and satisfying—a true morning treat. Want it sweeter? Increase the sugar by using flavored yogurt.

1. In blender or food processor, combine banana chunks, berries and orange juice. Purée until blended. Add yogurt; purée until smooth. If needed, add more juice to achieve desired consistency.

TIP

Don't throw out overripe bananas! Plan ahead for future smoothies; peel and freeze those black bananas in resealable plastic bags.

Peggy Beldon shared this recipe with me. She uses berries fresh from her garden.

Best Banana Bread

Makes 1 loaf

1½ cups all-purpose flour

1 teaspoon baking soda

½ teaspoon salt

3 large very ripe bananas

½ cup sour cream or plain yogurt

½ cup (1 stick) unsalted butter, melted, plus extra for pan

1 cup granulated sugar

2 large eggs

2 teaspoons vanilla extract

1 cup toasted walnuts, chopped

TIP

The riper the bananas, the better the banana flavor.

Toasting walnuts adds a nice crunch to this super-moist bread. Just spread the nuts out on a baking sheet and place in a preheated 350°F oven for 10 minutes.

1. Preheat oven to 350°F. Lightly butter bottom and sides of a 9-by-5-inch loaf pan; lightly coat with flour.

2. In a medium bowl, combine flour, baking soda and salt. In another bowl, mash bananas with sour cream or yogurt until blended. In a large mixing bowl with electric mixer on high speed, cream butter and sugar until light and fluffy. Add eggs and vanilla; beat until combined.

3. Fold banana mixture into batter until blended. Lightly fold in dry ingredients and walnuts until just combined. Batter will be chunky. Scrape batter into prepared pan. Bake about 1 hour, until golden brown and toothpick inserted in center comes out clean. Cool in pan for 5 minutes. Run a knife around edges of pan to loosen bread. Transfer to wire rack to cool completely.

Hearty Bran Apple Muffins

Simple and satisfying, these muffins make a healthy breakfast.

1. Preheat oven to 400°F. Lightly coat a standard muffin tin with cooking spray.
2. In food processor, pulse 2 cups of the cereal until finely ground. (Reserve remaining cereal.) In a large bowl, whisk flour, baking soda and salt until combined. In another large bowl, whisk egg and extra yolk until light in color. Whisk in brown sugar, honey or molasses and vanilla, then melted butter. Whisk in yogurt until combined. Fold in ground cereal until blended.
3. Gently fold in flour mixture, unground cereal and apples just until batter is combined. Do not overmix. Drop batter into prepared muffin cups. Batter should fill cups and mound on top. Sprinkle cinnamon-sugar over top of muffins.
4. Bake 15 to 20 minutes, until muffins are golden brown and a toothpick inserted in center comes out with a few crumbs. Cool in pan 5 minutes. Run a knife around muffin edges to release from pan. Transfer to wire rack to cool.

Makes 12 muffins

2½ cups All-Bran cereal

1¾ cups all-purpose flour

2 teaspoons baking soda

½ teaspoon salt

1 large egg

1 large egg yolk

¾ cup light brown sugar

2 tablespoons honey or molasses

1 teaspoon vanilla extract

6 tablespoons (¾ stick) unsalted butter, melted

1¾ cups plain yogurt or buttermilk

1 small apple, peeled and cut into chunks

¾ cup granulated sugar tossed with 2 tablespoons ground cinnamon

My friend Helen claims these will keep you regular as clockwork.

Breakfast Casserole with Bacon and Cheddar

Serves 6

8 ounces bacon

½ medium onion, chopped

1 red bell pepper, chopped

2 tablespoons all-purpose flour

1½ cups whole milk

1 pound frozen shredded hash brown potatoes

½ cup snipped fresh chives

1¼ cups shredded sharp cheddar cheese

TIP

The easiest way to cut fresh chives is to snip them with scissors.

This is a great winter weekend brunch dish.

1. Preheat oven to 350°F. Butter an 8-inch-square glass baking dish.
2. Cook bacon in a large heavy skillet over medium-high heat until crisp. Remove slices; drain on a paper-towel-lined plate. In same skillet over medium-low heat, cook onion and pepper in bacon drippings 8 minutes, until softened, stirring often.
3. Reduce heat under skillet to low. Stir in flour. Slowly pour in milk, ½ cup at a time, stirring to incorporate smoothly with the flour. Cook until mixture thickens and comes to a simmer, about 3 minutes, stirring often. Crumble bacon into mixture.
4. Evenly spread potatoes in prepared dish. Top with half of the chives, 1 cup of the cheese and the vegetable-bacon mixture. Sprinkle with the remaining ¼ cup cheese. Bake 40 minutes, until potatoes are tender. Sprinkle with remaining chives before cutting into squares.

Grace told me Cliff likes this best with pepper bacon. But it's your choice.

Cowboy Eggs with Smoky Black Beans and Lime-Avocado Salsa

Chipotle chilies lend a smoky flavor to the black bean sauce in this hearty breakfast. Chipotles are canned in adobo, a spicy tomato sauce. They are available at Latin American markets, specialty foods stores and many supermarkets. Be sure to seed the chile before adding it to the sauce.

1. Warm 1 tablespoon oil in a large nonstick skillet over medium heat. Add onion; cook 5 minutes, until softened, stirring often. Add cumin; cook 30 seconds. Stir in tomatoes with juice, beans, and chilies; bring to a simmer. Reduce heat; simmer 6 minutes, until most of the liquid is absorbed, stirring often.

2. In a medium bowl, combine avocado, cilantro and lime juice. Season with salt and pepper.

3. Warm remaining 1 tablespoon oil in another large nonstick skillet over medium-high heat until hot. Crack eggs into skillet; fry about 2½ minutes, until whites are just set but yolks are still soft. Season with salt and pepper.

4. Meanwhile, wrap tortillas in paper towel and warm in microwave. Set one tortilla on each of 4 plates. Divide bean mixture among tortillas. Top each with 1 fried egg; sprinkle with cheese. Serve with avocado salsa.

Serves 4

2 tablespoons vegetable oil, divided

1 small onion, chopped

1 tablespoon ground cumin

1 15-ounce can diced tomatoes in juice

1 15-ounce can black beans, drained and rinsed

1 canned chipotle chile packed in adobo sauce, seeded and chopped (about 2 teaspoons)

2 medium avocados, peeled, pitted and diced

½ cup chopped fresh cilantro

3 tablespoons fresh lime juice

Salt and pepper, to taste

4 large eggs

4 small (6-inch) flour tortillas

½ cup grated Monterey Jack cheese or sharp cheddar cheese

TIP

Save time by substituting 1¼ cups prepared salsa for the onion and tomatoes in the sauce.

Buttermilk Hotcakes with Blueberries

Cornmeal adds a bit of lightness and a delicate crunch to these pancakes. Frozen blueberries work just as well as fresh here.

1. In a large bowl, stir flour, cornmeal, sugar, baking powder, baking soda and salt until blended. In a medium bowl, whisk eggs, buttermilk and melted butter until combined. Pour buttermilk mixture into dry ingredients, stir just until smooth.

2. Preheat oven to 250°F. Lightly coat a heavy large skillet with oil; warm over medium heat. Drop batter by ¼ cupfuls into skillet. Sprinkle each pancake with 1 tablespoon blueberries. Cook pancakes about 2 minutes per side, until bottoms are golden brown. Transfer pancakes to large baking sheet; place in oven to keep warm. Repeat with remaining batter and blueberries, adding more oil to skillet as necessary.

Makes about 12

¾ cup all-purpose flour

¾ cup yellow cornmeal

2 tablespoons granulated sugar

½ teaspoon baking powder

½ teaspoon baking soda

½ teaspoon salt

2 large eggs

1¼ cups buttermilk

3 tablespoons butter, melted

Vegetable oil, for cooking

1–1½ cups fresh blueberries or frozen blueberries, thawed

An old family recipe my mother passed on to me. Much tastier than those prepared mixes.

> **TIP**
>
> These hotcakes are substantial enough to serve at dinner. Just substitute crumbled bacon and cheddar cheese for the blueberries. Top with sliced scallions and serve with sautéed onions and bell peppers.

Honey Nut Granola

Makes 10 cups

6 cups old-fashioned or quick oats

2 cups chopped nuts, any kind

1 cup sweetened coconut flakes

1 teaspoon ground cinnamon

¼ teaspoon salt

1 cup honey or maple syrup

2 cups dried cranberries, raisins or chopped dates

TIP

Warming the honey makes it easier to blend it into the oat mixture.

Add your family's favorite nuts and dried fruit to this easy recipe. Since granola can burn quickly, keep an eye on the cereal as it bakes.

1. Preheat oven to 325°F. In a large bowl, combine oats, nuts, coconut, cinnamon and salt. In a small cup, heat honey or maple syrup in microwave just until warm. Fold honey or maple syrup into oat mixture, stirring to coat well.

2. Evenly spread granola on two large, rimmed baking sheets. Place in oven and bake 25 to 30 minutes, carefully stirring granola often so it doesn't burn. Rotate pans after stirring. Granola is done when it seems lightly browned, mostly dry and no longer sticky. Let granola cool 15 minutes on baking sheets; pour into large bowl. Stir in dried fruit. Press mixture into bowl with back of a spoon; this will form some clumps. Let cool completely before sealing into an airtight container.

Ham and Cheese Stuffed Omelet

This savory satisfying omelet is a great way to start the day—
or a comforting light dinner.

1. Melt butter in an 8- or 9-inch nonstick skillet over medium
   heat. Meanwhile, in a large bowl, whisk eggs, salt and pepper
   until frothy.
2. Once pan is hot, add eggs; let sit for 3 seconds, until edges
   begin to set. Using a spatula, draw cooked egg to center of pan.
   Tilt pan so uncooked egg runs to bare spots. Repeat process
   all around edge of pan until omelet is just set.
3. Sprinkle ham and cheese evenly over half of omelet. Cook
   10 seconds, or until desired doneness. Run spatula around
   pan to loosen edges. Jerk the pan sharply to move entire omelet.
   Tilt pan, resting edge of pan on serving plate. Gently slide
   omelet onto plate, using spatula to fold omelet in half. Sprinkle
   with chives and serve hot.

Serves 2

1 tablespoon unsalted butter

5 large eggs

Salt and pepper, to taste

¼ cup diced cooked ham

¼ cup shredded Monterey Jack cheese

2 tablespoons snipped fresh chives

• TIP

Omelets cook best if you wait until the pan is hot before adding the eggs.

A Sunday favorite after Pastor Flemming's sermons.

Sunday Sour Cream Coffee Cake

Makes 1 cake

TOPPING

1 cup chopped toasted walnuts

¾ cup light brown sugar

1 tablespoon ground cinnamon

CAKE

4 cups all-purpose flour

2 teaspoons baking powder

2 teaspoons baking soda

1 teaspoon salt

1 cup (2 sticks) unsalted butter, at room temperature

2 cups granulated sugar

4 large eggs

1 tablespoon vanilla extract

2 cups sour cream

If you make this cake once, you'll make it a hundred times—it's that delicious.

1. Preheat oven to 350°F. Butter a large (10-cup) tube pan, preferably with a removable bottom. Dust pan with flour. In a small bowl, combine nuts, brown sugar and cinnamon for topping and set aside.

2. In a medium bowl, combine flour, baking powder, baking soda and salt. In a large bowl with electric mixer on high speed, cream butter and granulated sugar until light and fluffy. Add eggs, one at a time, until blended, and stir in vanilla. Alternately add sour cream and dry ingredients, starting and ending with the dry ingredients.

3. Spoon half the batter into the prepared pan. Sprinkle half of the topping over the batter. Spoon remaining batter into pan. Sprinkle with remaining topping.

4. Bake 1 hour 5 minutes, until a toothpick inserted in center comes out clean. Run a knife around the edges to loosen from pan. Remove pan sides. Run a knife under cake to loosen from pan bottom. Carefully lift cake out of pan. Transfer to wire rack to cool.

TIP

You can substitute plain yogurt or low-fat sour cream for the sour cream.

Corn Muffins with Raspberries

Makes 12

1⅓ cups yellow cornmeal

1 cup all-purpose flour

⅓ cup granulated sugar

1 tablespoon baking powder

½ teaspoon salt

1 cup plus 2 tablespoons buttermilk

½ cup (1 stick) unsalted butter, melted

2 tablespoons molasses

1 large egg plus 1 large egg yolk, lightly beaten

1 cup fresh raspberries or frozen raspberries, thawed

TIP

Not in the mood for muffins? You can easily make this recipe into cornbread. Just pour the batter into a greased, heavy 9-inch skillet and bake for about 25 minutes. (see page 191 for another cornbread recipe)

These are best eaten the day they are baked; the juicy berries will make the muffins soggy if left too long.

1. Preheat oven to 375°F. Lightly coat a standard muffin tin with cooking spray.
2. In a large bowl, whisk cornmeal, flour, sugar, baking powder and salt. Using a wooden spoon, fold in buttermilk, melted butter, molasses and beaten eggs until blended. Let mixture stand 10 minutes to absorb liquid. Gently fold in raspberries.
3. Drop batter into prepared muffin cups. Bake 15 minutes, until toothpick inserted in center comes out clean. Cool in pan 5 minutes. Run a knife around muffin edges to release from pan. Transfer to wire rack to cool.

Jack published this recipe of mine in the Chronicle. Lots of people have told me how much they like it.

Homemade Cinnamon Rolls

Although there are a lot of steps to this recipe, the joy of creating homemade cinnamon rolls makes it worth the effort.

1. In a glass measuring cup, microwave milk and butter until butter melts.
2. In a large bowl with electric mixer on low speed, combine yeast and warm water; let sit for 5 minutes. Beat in ½ cup granulated sugar and eggs at low speed until blended. Beat in salt, warm milk mixture and 2 cups of flour until blended, about 1 minute. Switch to dough hook attachment. Add 1¼ cups flour, and knead at medium-low speed, adding up to ½ cup additional flour if dough is sticky. Mix until dough is smooth and pulls away from sides of bowl, about 10 minutes.
3. Turn dough onto a lightly floured countertop. Transfer dough to a large, lightly oiled plastic bowl. Cover bowl with plastic wrap; let dough rise until double in size, about 2½ hours. Punch down center of dough. (At this point, dough can be covered and refrigerated overnight.)
4. Turn dough onto a lightly floured countertop. Let dough rest 10 minutes. Lightly butter a 13-by-9-inch baking pan.
5. For filling: In a small bowl, mix ⅓ cup granulated sugar and cinnamon.
6. Using a floured rolling pin, roll dough into a 12-by-16-inch rectangle. Brush with milk and sprinkle with cinnamon-sugar filling, leaving a ½-inch border along one of the long sides. Roll, beginning with the long side of the rectangle opposite the ½-inch border. Using fingertips, seal edges firmly to form a seam. (Do not seal ends.) Using a serrated knife, cut dough log into 12 even rolls and arrange in prepared pan.
7. Cover pan with plastic wrap; let dough rise until double in size, about 1 hour. Preheat oven to 350°F. Set oven rack to center position.
8. Bake 25 to 30 minutes, until golden brown. Invert rolls onto wire rack; cool 20 minutes.
9. For the icing: In a small bowl, whisk confectioners' sugar, milk and vanilla until smooth. Place rack over a piece of wax paper; reinvert rolls onto rack. Using a spoon, drizzle icing over rolls with spoon.

Makes 12

½ cup whole milk

4 tablespoons (½ stick) unsalted butter, cut into chunks

1 package (2¼ teaspoons) active dry yeast

½ cup warm water

½ cup granulated sugar

2 large eggs

1 teaspoon salt

3¼ cups all-purpose flour, plus extra for rolling

FILLING

⅓ cup granulated sugar

4 teaspoons ground cinnamon

Milk for brushing

ICING

1 cup confectioners' sugar

2 tablespoons whole milk

½ teaspoon vanilla extract

TIP

If you like, after the first rise (Step 3), cover the dough and refrigerate overnight. Continue the recipe the next day.

Shown on page 11

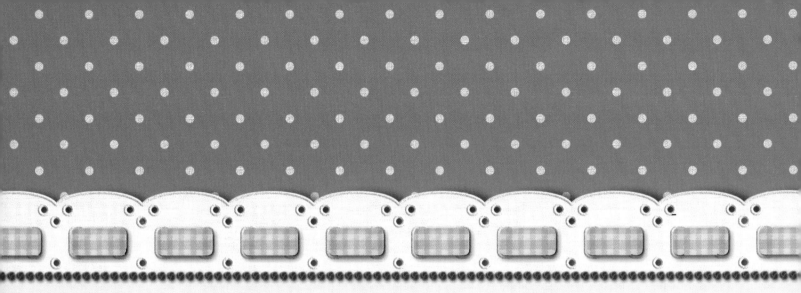

Lunch

at **204 ROSEWOOD LANE** *with*

Grace Sherman Harding

My daughter, Olivia, and Grace Harding have always been best friends. In grade school they were both in Girl Scouts and attended summer camp together, and as teenagers they were inseparable. Many an afternoon was spent in my kitchen, making cookies for their boyfriends, bake sales and various class functions. Grace is a natural; she loves to cook even more than Olivia does.

Grace married her high school sweetheart, Dan Sherman, right after graduation. They were far too young, of course, although Clyde and I were married when I was even younger— but that was during the war years and marriage at sixteen or seventeen wasn't uncommon. Pretty soon I knew why Grace and Dan had rushed to the altar.

Grace was pregnant with Maryellen. While Olivia went off to college, Grace became a wife and mother. In order to support his young family Dan enlisted in the army and left for Vietnam. Their younger daughter, Kelly, was born after his return.

Although Olivia never said anything to me, I had the feeling that Grace's marriage wasn't a happy one. But she persevered and I do believe she loved Dan, although he could certainly be difficult. I admire the fact that she made the best of things. I also admire Dan for the way he took over much of the housework while Grace went back to school and got her librarian's degree. And no doubt about it, his girls loved him. I suspect that Dan was a better father than he was a husband.

Because she was often busy with her studies, I gave Grace a number of recipes that were quick and easy to prepare. My homemade soup recipes, in particular, became popular with her family through the years.

The Chicken Noodle Soup, for example, originated in my mother's kitchen. It's good for what ails you, as she liked to say. The Tomato Soup with Basil was contributed by my dear friend Bess. She often brings it to the Senior Center potlucks, and I've seen grown men squabble over the last bowl.

But back to Grace… I don't think anyone was more surprised than me when Dan Sherman went missing—what was it? Eight years ago? Grace got home from work one afternoon and Dan wasn't there. He'd apparently vanished into thin air—no message, no phone call, nothing. More than a year passed before anyone learned what had happened to him. It turns out he'd gone deep into the woods and taken his own life. I feel sad whenever I think about him.

Grace was beside herself with worry that whole year, and the girls, too. Kelly, who was pregnant, convinced herself that Dan would return in time to see his grandchild. Needless to say, he didn't, and it broke the poor girl's heart. Eventually they all found peace with Dan's death but it took a long time—and a lot of compassion.

Then Grace met Cliff Harding. I feel personally responsible for that, although I'm no matchmaker. It just seemed that they were two lonely people who had a lot to offer each other. Although the course of true love didn't run smooth (and I'm sorry to tell you that was mainly because of my son, Will), Cliff and Grace did end up together. In fact, they eloped in San Francisco. They told me how much they enjoyed visiting

Chinatown, which is one reason I've included some of our favorite Chinese recipes. Spicy Hot Sauce Chicken Noodles are downright addictive, according to Cliff, and the Wonton Soup is a perennial favorite.

I've never seen Grace happier. After the wedding (such as it was), she moved into Cliff's place in Olalla, where he has a small horse ranch, and now rents out her home on Rosewood Lane. She's brought a real sense of warmth to his house, which desperately needed a woman's touch. I can picture her in that huge kitchen with a big pot of soup simmering on the stove, making Grilled Cheese Sandwiches for Cliff and whoever might be visiting.

The next time you have people over for lunch, try some of these recipes, courtesy of Grace (and me!).

Spicy Hot Sauce Chicken Noodles

Serves 4

4 scallions, thinly sliced

2 cloves garlic, minced

⅓ cup soy sauce

⅓ cup rice-wine vinegar

2 tablespoons brown sugar

1 tablespoon fresh lime juice

¼ teaspoon red-pepper flakes, as needed

4 boneless, skinless chicken breasts, thinly sliced crosswise

6 ounces Chinese rice noodles or thin spaghetti, broken in half if long

1 tablespoon vegetable oil, such as peanut

2 carrots, sliced into ribbons with a vegetable peeler

1 cucumber, halved lengthwise and thinly sliced crosswise

Fresh mint and chopped peanuts, for garnish

TIP

For a prettier carrot slice, use a vegetable peeler to create ribbons of orange.

This versatile dish tastes great hot, warm or cold.

1. In a medium bowl, combine scallions, garlic, soy sauce, vinegar, brown sugar, lime juice and pepper flakes. Remove and set aside about half of this sauce. Add chicken strips to remaining sauce in bowl. Marinate for at least 30 minutes or refrigerate overnight.

2. Cook noodles according to package directions. Drain; rinse with cold water to stop the cooking. Transfer to a platter.

3. Warm oil in a large skillet over medium-high heat. Lift chicken from marinade and stir-fry chicken in 2 batches, about 2 minutes per batch, until cooked through. Discard marinade. Using tongs, place chicken on top of noodles.

4. Add carrots and cucumber to chicken and noodles. Drizzle with reserved dressing if desired and gently toss to coat. Scatter mint and peanuts over platter.

Be careful with those red pepper flakes. Food isn't supposed to hurt!

Anytime Tomato Soup with Fresh Basil and Swiss Cheese Pita Croutons

A homey from-the-pantry soup made from ingredients you probably have on hand.

1. For croutons: Preheat oven to 350°F. Slice pitas in half crosswise; separate to form 8 semicircles. Arrange on a baking sheet and sprinkle the rough sides of the pita with the cheese; season with salt. Bake 13 minutes, until golden and crispy. Cut or break into 2-inch wedges.

2. For soup: Melt butter in a medium saucepan over low heat. Add shallots; cook 5 minutes, until softened, stirring often. Stir in garlic and bay leaf; cook 30 seconds. Stir in tomatoes and their juices and brown sugar. Bring to a boil. Reduce heat; simmer 10 minutes, stirring occasionally and mashing tomatoes against the side of the bowl. Remove bay leaf.

3. Transfer mixture to a blender. Purée until smooth. Return to pot over medium heat. Stir in broth and warm through. Season to taste with salt and pepper. Garnish servings with chopped basil and pita croutons.

TIP

Want cream of tomato soup? Stir in 2 tablespoons heavy cream in the last few minutes of warming the soup.

Serves 6

CROUTONS

2 pita pockets

½ cup finely shredded Swiss cheese

Salt, to taste

SOUP

2 tablespoons butter

2 shallots, chopped

3 cloves garlic, minced

1 bay leaf

2 28-ounce cans whole tomatoes

2 tablespoons brown sugar

1 cup reduced-sodium chicken broth

Salt and pepper, to taste

Chopped fresh basil, for garnish

Windy Weather Grilled Cheese Sandwiches

Makes 4

1¼ cups shredded cheddar cheese

¾ cup shredded Monterey Jack cheese

8 slices white sandwich bread

4 tablespoons unsalted butter, melted

TIP

For best flavor, shred a block of cheese rather than using preshredded cheese.

There's no greater comfort food than the classic Grilled Cheese—satisfyingly crunchy on the outside and oozing, melting cheese on the inside. Although Monterey Jack cheese adds a depth of cheese flavor, purists can use all Cheddar in this homey sandwich.

1. Preheat oven to 250°F. In a medium bowl, toss cheeses together until combined. Lay four bread slices out on a baking sheet; lightly coat one side of each slice with half of the butter. Flip bread; sprinkle evenly with cheese and top with second bread slice to make four sandwiches. Lightly coat top slices with remaining butter.

2. Warm a large nonstick skillet over medium-low heat. Place 2 sandwiches in skillet; cook 5 minutes, until golden, pressing down on sandwiches evenly with a spatula. Flip; cook 3 minutes, until golden. Transfer sandwiches to baking sheet; place baking sheet in oven to keep warm. Cook remaining sandwiches.

Every once in a while I slip in some swiss cheese to give this an international flavor.

Summer Minestrone with Pesto Purée

Serves 8 to 10

1 cup dried cannellini or Great Northern beans

2 bay leaves

6 cloves garlic, divided

2 tablespoons olive oil

4 cups reduced-sodium chicken broth

3 leeks, white parts thinly sliced and washed

3 carrots, sliced

2 medium boiling potatoes, such as Yukon Gold, unpeeled and diced

2 small zucchini, diced

2 large ripe tomatoes, chopped

2 cups green beans, trimmed and cut into 1-inch lengths

Salt, to taste

BASIL PESTO PURÉE

2 cloves garlic, smashed

2 tablespoons pine nuts or chopped walnuts

Salt and pepper, to taste

4 cups loosely packed basil leaves, washed

½ cup extra-virgin olive oil

½ cup grated Parmesan cheese

Shown on page 2

This soup is based on the classic Provençal Soupe au Pistou. Bright summer vegetables combine in light soup, garnished with a swirl of basil pesto purée.

1. For soup: In medium saucepan, combine cannellini beans, bay leaves, 2 crushed garlic cloves and 8 cups water. Bring to a simmer; let cook, partially covered, for 50 minutes, until beans are tender. Strain; reserving broth and beans separately. Combine bean broth and chicken broth; add water to equal 10 cups.

2. Warm oil in large saucepan or soup pot over medium heat. Add leeks, carrots, potatoes and remaining 4 cloves garlic, chopped. Cook 15 minutes, stirring often. Add reserved broth and water; bring to a simmer. Cook 30 minutes, stirring occasionally. Add zucchini; cook 20 minutes, stirring occasionally. Add cannellini beans, tomatoes and green beans; cook 10 minutes until vegetables are tender and soup is warmed through.

3. For basil pesto purée: In blender or food processor, purée garlic, nuts and a sprinkle of salt until finely chopped. Add basil and oil; blend until smooth. Add cheese and blend until combined. Taste and add salt if needed.

4. Serve warm soup garnished with a dollop of basil pesto purée. Season to taste with salt and pepper.

TIP

You'll have leftover basil pesto purée. Refrigerate, tightly covered, and use as a pasta sauce.

Italian Deli Panini

Black olive paste, also called tapenade, is a tangy dip or sandwich spread made from olives, garlic and oil.

1. Preheat an electric panini press or indoor grill according to appliance directions.
2. Cut each foccacia piece in half horizontally to make 4 pieces.
3. Brush uncut sides of each bread slice with oil. Lay slices on countertop, oiled-side down. Spread half of the cut sides with olive paste, then layer with salami, provolone, peppers and arugula. Top with remaining bread slices. Press sandwiches together and place on press or grill. Cook according to appliance directions or until bread is toasted and cheese melted.

I've always enjoyed anything Italian. You've got to love a country that has so many varieties of pasta.

Serves 2

2 slices foccacia, each about 4 inches square

Olive oil

Black olive paste

4 ounces sliced salami

4 ounces sliced provolone

2 roasted red peppers, thinly sliced

Arugula leaves

TIP

Spread any leftover tapenade on crackers or crisp toast as an appetizer or snack.

Panini Marguerita

Foccacia is a thick rectangular Italian flatbread. It's now available in many supermarket bakeries or specialty stores.

1. Preheat an electric panini press or indoor grill according to appliance directions.
2. Cut each foccacia piece in half horizontally to make 4 pieces.
3. Brush uncut sides of each bread slice with oil. Lay slices on countertop, oiled-side down. Spread half of the cut sides with mayonnaise. Layer tomato, basil and mozzarella; season with salt and pepper. Top with remaining bread slice. Press sandwiches together and place on press or grill. Cook according to appliance directions or until bread is toasted and cheese melted.

Serves 2

2 slices foccacia, each about 4 inches square

Olive oil

Mayonnaise

1 large tomato, thinly sliced

Fresh basil leaves

1 cup shredded mozzarella cheese

Salt and pepper, to taste

> **TIP**
>
> If you can't find foccacia, substitute a fat Italian loaf.

This goes even better when served with a margarita!

Creamy Tarragon Chicken Salad

Serves 6

2 pounds boneless, skinless chicken breast halves (about 4)

8 ounces sugar snap peas, trimmed

½ cup sour cream (regular or reduced fat)

½ cup mayonnaise

3 tablespoons fresh lemon juice

2 teaspoons Dijon mustard

2 stalks celery, thinly sliced

2 tablespoons minced red onion

¼ cup finely chopped fresh tarragon

Salt, to taste

This is a lovely salad for a light lunch on a warm summer day. Double the recipe and it's perfect party fare.

1. Trim excess fat from chicken. Place chicken in medium heavy saucepan; cover with water and place over medium-high heat. Bring to a simmer; cook 10 minutes, or until chicken is just cooked. Transfer to bowl; let cool. Shred into 1-inch strips.

2. Bring water to a boil in medium saucepan over high heat. Add peas; cook 3 minutes, until tender-crisp. Drain and rinse with cold water.

3. In a medium bowl, combine sour cream, mayonnaise, lemon juice and mustard. Add chicken strips, peas, celery, onion and tarragon. Season with salt.

TIP

Fresh herbs last longer if they are stored correctly. First, remove any rubber bands from the bunch, then trim off any woody stems. Put the unwashed bunch, stems down, in a tall glass. Add water just to cover the stems. Cover loosely with a plastic bag and refrigerate for up to 5 days.

Don't tell anyone, but I have been known to buy one of those roasted chickens from the grocery!

Turkey, Provolone and Garden-Vegetable Wrap

S callion cream cheese adds a burst of flavor to this hearty sandwich. Check out the varieties of cream cheese now available in the dairy case—there's no excuse for a boring wrap!

1. Lay tortilla on countertop. Spread cream cheese on tortilla. Layer turkey, cheese, cucumber, spinach and sprouts. Tightly roll up tortilla; slice in half diagonally.

Serves 2

1 large plain or spinach flour wrap (or flour tortilla)

2 tablespoons scallion cream cheese

4 ounces sliced roast turkey

2 ounces sliced provolone cheese

8 thin cucumber slices (about ¼ of a cucumber)

Handful baby spinach leaves

½ cup alfalfa sprouts

TIP

Look for ready-made wraps at your market. Since this sandwich is stuffed full, you need a strong wrap to hold it all.

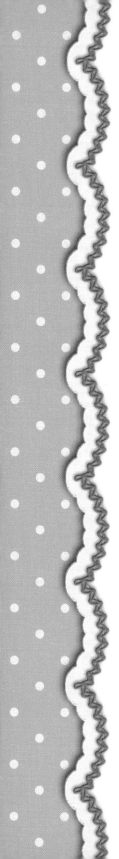

Broccoli and Cheese Soup in a Bread Bowl

Serves 4

2 tablespoons unsalted butter

1 small onion, chopped

Salt and pepper, to taste

1 clove garlic, chopped

1 teaspoon chopped fresh thyme

3 tablespoons all-purpose flour

4 cups reduced-sodium chicken broth

1 pound broccoli (about 2 heads), stems thinly sliced and florets cut small

½ cup heavy cream

1 cup shredded cheddar cheese

4 small round bread loaves (4–5 ounces each)

Olive oil

TIP

Look in the bakery section of your supermarket for bread rounds—about 5 ounces in weight—to make the bowls.

Haven't you always wanted to make your own soup in a bread bowl, like in restaurants? Now you can.

1. Melt butter in a medium saucepan over medium heat. Add onion; cook 5 minutes, until softened, stirring often. Add garlic, thyme, salt and pepper; cook 1 minute, stirring. Sprinkle in flour, stirring constantly until incorporated. Slowly pour in broth, ½ cup at a time, stirring to blend. Add broccoli; cook 10 minutes, until tender.

2. Using an immersion blender, purée soup until smooth. (Or transfer soup to a blender; blend until smooth.)

3. Return soup to pot; add cream and cheese and warm over low heat, stirring.

4. For bread bowl: Preheat oven to 400°F. Using a serrated knife, slice a thin circle off the top of each round. Lift off the circle; use your fingers to pull out the soft insides of the bread, leaving at least a ½ inch of bread around the sides and bottom of the loaf. Set the loaves on a baking sheet and drizzle olive oil into each cavity; spread the oil to coat the inside. Bake rounds about 10 minutes, or until crusty and golden. Ladle warm soup into bowls and serve immediately.

August Corn Chowder

Made in August, this soup highlights the sweetness of just-picked fresh corn. But it's still good made other times of the year using a 16-ounce bag of frozen corn.

1. Melt butter in medium saucepan or soup pot over medium heat. Add onion; cook 5 minutes, stirring often. Add garlic, thyme, salt and pepper; cook 1 minute, stirring. Add broth and 1½ cups water; bring to a simmer.
2. Add potatoes to simmering broth; cook 20 minutes, until cooked through. Stir in corn kernels and tomatoes; cook 15 minutes.
3. Remove from heat; stir in vinegar. Garnish servings with sour cream and tarragon.

My garden's small these days, so I pick up fresh corn at the Farmer's Market.

Serves 4

2 tablespoons unsalted butter

1 medium onion or 2 shallots, finely chopped

3 cloves garlic, minced

1 teaspoon dried whole thyme or 2 teaspoons chopped fresh thyme

Salt and pepper, to taste

3½ cups reduced-sodium chicken broth

1½ cups water

4 medium boiling potatoes, such as Yukon Gold, unpeeled and diced

5 ears corn, kernels scraped off

2 medium beefsteak tomatoes, chopped

1 tablespoon red-wine vinegar

Sour cream and chopped fresh tarragon, for garnish

TIP

Substitute always-available cherry tomatoes in the winter months, when beefsteak tomatoes aren't available.

Homemade (with Help) Chicken Noodle Soup

Serves 6

2 tablespoons olive oil

1 small onion, finely chopped

2 large carrots, peeled and very thinly sliced

1 stalk celery, thinly sliced

1 teaspoon fresh thyme or ½ teaspoon dried whole thyme

8 cups reduced-sodium chicken broth

3 cups shredded meat from a purchased rotisserie chicken

2 cups water

3 ounces wide egg noodles (about 1 cup dry)

¾ cup frozen peas (about half of a 10-ounce box)

Salt and pepper, to taste

Chopped fresh parsley leaves, for garnish

TIP

Because the recipe calls for a large amount of chicken broth, use the reduced-sodium variety.

This classic soup is made easy by using a precooked rotisserie chicken. You'll need one small roasted chicken for the soup.

1. Warm oil in a large saucepan or soup pot over medium heat. Add onion, carrots, celery and thyme; cook 8 minutes, until softened, stirring occasionally. Pour in broth, shredded chicken and about 2 cups water. Bring to a simmer; let cook 5 minutes, until vegetables are tender and flavors combine.
2. Add noodles and peas; cook about 8 minutes, until noodles are tender. Season with salt and pepper and garnish with parsley.

My mother's recipe, which I've modified (and simplified) through the years.

Wonton Soup with Pork and Bok Choy

Making wontons is a fun activity for the whole family. Look for dumpling skins (sometimes called wonton wrappers) in the refrigerated section of your supermarket or at Asian markets.

1. Bring a medium saucepan of water to a boil. Add salt and bok choy stems; cook 1 minute. Add bok choy leaves; cook 1 minute. Drain; run under cold water to stop cooking. Transfer bok choy to a cutting board; press with a clean dishcloth to squeeze dry. Coarsely chop.

2. In a large bowl, combine bok choy, pork, scallions, ginger, soy sauce, sesame oil, sugar and vinegar until combined.

3. Place one wonton wrapper on the countertop. Spoon about 2 teaspoons of the filling in the center of dumpling. Dip your finger in a bowl of warm water and moisten the edges of the dumpling. Fold the wrapper over the filling to make a half-moon shape, pressing the wet sides together to seal. Gently bend dumpling to make the classic crescent shape (this looks sort of like a nurse's cap). Repeat until all dumplings are finished, storing finished dumplings on a baking sheet under a damp dish towel to keep them from drying out.

4. For soup: In a medium saucepan, combine broth, scallions, garlic and 4 cups of water. Bring to a simmer over medium heat. Add wontons and snow peas and simmer, until filling is just cooked through, about 5 minutes. The dumplings will rise to the top when done.

5. Ladle the soup into serving bowls; garnish with a dash of sesame oil.

* TIP
> If baby bok choy is unavailable, regular-sized bok choy is a fine substitute.

Serves 4

WONTONS

Salt

1 head baby bok choy, coarsely chopped, stems and leaves separated

2/3 pound ground pork

2 scallions, minced

1 tablespoon peeled and minced fresh ginger

1 tablespoon soy sauce

1 tablespoon Asian sesame oil

2 teaspoons granulated sugar

1 teaspoon rice-wine vinegar

36 dumpling skins or wonton wrappers

SOUP

4 cups reduced-sodium chicken broth

2 scallions, minced

1 clove garlic, minced

4 cups water

6 ounces snow peas, trimmed

Asian sesame oil

Tea

at **6 RAINIER DRIVE** *and the*
VICTORIAN TEA ROOM *with*

Justine Gunderson

If it wasn't for Justine I probably wouldn't have assembled all these recipes. My granddaughter asked me to compile my favorites when she decided to open the Victorian Tea Room. Needless to say, I was honored by her request.

As any grandmother does, I cherish my grandchildren. However there's a unique bond between my only granddaughter and me. Tragedy struck Justine's life early when her twin brother, Jordan, drowned. I'm not exaggerating when I tell you that Jordan's death changed her life forever. It affected all of us, but it touched her more deeply than anyone else. That stands to reason, of course, since they were so close—and because she was with him when it happened.

I didn't mean to start this chapter with such sad thoughts, especially since my granddaughter's experienced so many positive changes in the past few years. The day she married Seth Gunderson was surely one of the happiest of her life—her mother's and mine, too.

Justine and Seth are well suited and have a solid marriage. I don't mean to suggest that everything's gone smoothly for them because I know it hasn't. But they've worked out their problems, some of them caused (*deliberately* caused!) by a former boyfriend of Justine's.

The tea room has replaced The Lighthouse, the restaurant Seth and Justine used to own and which they lost to arson. They'd worked long and hard to make it

the success it quickly became. There *are* other restaurants in town (even if they aren't quite as elegant as the Lighthouse) but the tea room is one of a kind. The moment she mentioned it, I knew this was exactly what Cedar Cove needed. And now the Victorian Tea Room is thriving.

I hate to say it, but the Lighthouse was perhaps *too* successful, and I suspect that contributed to their marital woes. Justine's hours are a lot more reasonable these days, which is a good thing, considering that they have a family (which is about to grow in size).

Justine took my advice about the menu and has included a selection of savory dishes, like a delicious Broccoli Quiche with Ham and Gruyère, and desserts as well. The Chocolate Chip Oatmeal and Coconut Cookies are Sheriff Troy Davis's all-time favorite. His late wife, Sandy (God rest her soul), gave me that recipe years ago. Justine has much to thank Sheriff Davis for, and I believe she put these cookies on the afternoon tea menu specifically as a tribute to him.

And then there's the Pumpkin Tea Cake, which I promise will melt in your mouth. You won't be surprised to learn that this recipe's from Peggy Beldon who serves it at the B and B she and her husband run. I'm sure her secret is the pumpkins she grows in her huge garden. I've never gone to the trouble Peggy does; I use canned pumpkin instead, and in my humble opinion it's *almost* as good.

A word of advice about the Super Fudge Brownies. If you're watching your sugar, as so many of us must now, these should be saved for a special occasion. On second thought, a Friday afternoon or Sunday morning might be considered special enough. Justine recently told me that chocolate should be considered its own food group and I agree with her.

Of course, it's practically mandatory for a tea room to serve scones. The Honey-Walnut Scones are the ones I like best. I can't recall where I got the recipe; all I can say is that everyone loves these whenever I bake them. The Cheese and Herb variation scones are equally good, whether you serve them with breakfast, tea or brunch.

I know you'll enjoy reading these recipes—and they'll whet your appetite for lunch or an afternoon snack at the tea room. Make sure you tell Justine I sent you!

Confetti Crab Salad

Serves 4

½ cup mayonnaise

2 tablespoons fresh lemon juice

½ teaspoon mustard

1 scallion, thinly sliced

1 tablespoon chopped fresh dill

1 tablespoon chopped fresh tarragon

1 tablespoon chopped fresh parsley

Salt and pepper, to taste

1 pound lump crabmeat

1 small red bell pepper, diced

1 small yellow bell pepper, diced

1 avocado, peeled and diced

8–12 large lettuce leaves

TIP

Buy precooked crabmeat labeled jumbo, or lump, which is made of large chunks of meat from the body of the crustacean. It's usually sold at the fish counter in plastic or metal tubs.

Don't be put off by the number of ingredients in this recipe. Just chop everything up and stir it all together.

1. In a large bowl, whisk mayonnaise, lemon juice, mustard, scallions, all herbs, salt and pepper until blended.
2. Fold in crabmeat, then bell peppers and avocado. Season with salt and pepper. Arrange lettuce leaves on a large platter; top with crab salad.

Ben and I are especially fond of this salad on summer nights.

D.D.'s on the Cove Crab-Melt Sandwich

Serves 4

½ cup mayonnaise

2 tablespoons fresh lime juice

2 teaspoons mustard

2 tablespoons snipped fresh chives

Dash hot sauce

Salt and pepper, to taste

1 pound lump crabmeat

4 English muffins, split

4 tablespoons unsalted butter, at room temperature

1 cup shredded cheddar or Swiss cheese

4 tomato slices

TIP

Always pick over crabmeat to make sure there are no tiny shell pieces.

Bursting with lots of crabmeat, these warm sandwiches make a luxurious supper.

1. In large bowl, combine mayonnaise, lime juice, mustard, chives, hot sauce, salt and pepper until blended. Fold in crabmeat. Refrigerate mixture at least 30 minutes.

2. Preheat broiler. Lightly butter English muffins; toast until golden-brown. Lay four muffin halves, buttered-side up, on a baking sheet. Top each with a generous ½ cup of the crab mixture; sprinkle evenly with cheese. Broil muffins until cheese melts and crab is warmed through.

3. Top warm sandwiches with a tomato slice and remaining muffin tops.

White-Chocolate Chunk Oatmeal Cookies

Just for fun, the cookies are sprinkled with large grains of salt to offset the sweetness of the white chocolate. Omit the salt on top, if you like. You do need the salt in the cookie batter, however.

1. Preheat oven to 350°F. Line two baking sheets with parchment paper.
2. In a medium bowl, whisk flour, baking powder, baking soda and table salt.
3. In a large bowl with electric mixer on high speed, beat butter and both sugars until light and fluffy. Scrape down bowl with rubber spatula; add egg and vanilla and beat until blended. Scrape down bowl again. Slowly add flour mixture; mix until just incorporated. Stir in oats and white chocolate.
4. Drop dough by rounded tablespoons onto prepared sheets. Using fingertips, gently press down each ball to slightly flatten. Sprinkle a flake or two of coarse salt on each cookie.
5. Bake 14 minutes, until cookies are golden brown, rotating baking sheet halfway through. Transfer to wire rack to cool.

Makes 20 cookies

1 cup all-purpose flour

¾ teaspoon baking powder

½ teaspoon baking soda

¼ teaspoon table salt

14 tablespoons (1¾ sticks) unsalted butter, at room temperature

½ cup granulated sugar

½ cup brown sugar

1 large egg

2 teaspoons vanilla extract

2½ cups old-fashioned or quick oats

6 ounces good-quality white chocolate bar, chopped

½ teaspoon large-grain salt (like coarse sea salt or fleur de sel), for topping

White chocolate has always been my weakness. I save these for special occasions.

> **TIP**
>
> Use white chocolate bars or blocks; the packaged chips taste artificial and super-sweet.

Shown on page 233

Chef's Salad

A salad makes a hearty meal when it's chock-full of goodies like bacon, ham, turkey and cheese.

1. For the dressing: In a glass measuring cup, whisk all dressing ingredients until combined.
2. Cook bacon in a large heavy skillet over medium heat until crisp; drain on paper-towel-lined plate. Coarsely chop.
3. Stack turkey, ham and cheese slices; thinly slice stack to create strips of meat and cheese. In a large serving bowl, toss lettuce, bacon bits, meat and cheese strips and egg wedges with dressing.

What makes this a bit unusual is the dressing. According to Faith Beckwith, the dry mustard gives it punch.

Serves 4

DRESSING

½ cup buttermilk

2 tablespoons sour cream

1 tablespoon mayonnaise

½ teaspoon dry mustard

2 tablespoons fresh tarragon

Salt and pepper, to taste

SALAD

6 slices bacon

4 ounces sliced roast turkey

4 ounces sliced ham

4 ounces sliced Swiss cheese

1 large head Romaine lettuce, torn or chopped

4 hard-boiled eggs, peeled and cut into wedges

TIP

Add your favorite ingredients to make this salad your own. Some ideas: avocado, tomato, radishes, croutons.

Chocolate Chip, Oatmeal and Coconut Cookies

Makes 24 cookies

1¼ cups all-purpose flour

½ teaspoon baking soda

¼ teaspoon baking powder

¼ teaspoon salt

12 tablespoons (1½ sticks) unsalted butter, at room temperature

½ cup brown sugar

½ cup granulated sugar

1 large egg

1 egg yolk

2 teaspoons vanilla extract

1½ cups quick or old-fashioned oats

1 12-ounce bag semisweet chocolate chips

1 cup toasted pecans, chopped

1 cup sweetened coconut flakes

TIP

Substitute chopped almonds for the pecans and you'll get a cookie reminiscent of an old-time coconut-almond candy bar.

Chunky, chewy and chock-full of flavors, and a nice change of pace from the traditional chocolate-chipper.

1. Preheat oven to 350°F. Line two baking sheets with parchment paper.
2. In large mixing bowl with electric mixer, cream butter and both sugars until fluffy. Add egg, yolk and vanilla; beat until combined. Reduce speed to low; gradually add the flour mixture. Fold in oats, chocolate chips, nuts and coconut flakes until combined. Cover dough; refrigerate at least 1 hour
3. Spoon ¼ cup of dough about 2 inches apart onto prepared sheets. Bake 12 minutes, until just set. Edges will be only slightly browned. Do not overbake. Cool on baking sheet 5 minutes. Transfer to wire rack to cool completely.

Cookies are even more fun to bake with grandchildren— although I get fewer from a batch.

Giant Chocolate Peanut Butter Chip Cookies

Two great tastes combine in a cookie that brings out the kid in all of us. Serve with a tall glass of milk.

1. Preheat oven to 350°F. Line two baking sheets with parchment paper.
2. In large bowl with electric mixer on high speed, cream butter and sugar until blended. Add eggs; beat until blended. Beat in cocoa powder. Beat in flour, salt and baking powder until just combined. Fold in chocolate and peanut butter chips. Use a wooden spoon to gently turn the dough in bowl to ensure all ingredients are combined.
3. Drop dough by ⅓ cup craggy balls onto prepared sheets. Press down on balls to flatten slightly. Bake 16 to 18 minutes (16 minutes yields a very fudgy cookie). Let cool on pan for 5 minutes. Transfer to wire rack to cool completely.

Makes 18 cookies

1 cup (2 sticks) unsalted butter, at room temperature

1¼ cups granulated sugar

2 large eggs

½ cup cocoa powder

2½ cups all-purpose flour

¼ teaspoon salt

1 teaspoon baking powder

½ cup semisweet chocolate chips or chunks

1 12-ounce bag peanut butter chips

TIP

Take the cookies out of the oven when they still seem a bit underbaked and soft in the middle.

Pumpkin Tea Cake with Honey Cream

Makes 1 loaf

LOAF

2½ cups all-purpose flour

2 teaspoons baking soda

½ teaspoon salt

1 tablespoon plus 1 teaspoon pumpkin-pie spice

2 large eggs

1¼ cups granulated sugar

½ cup (1 stick) unsalted butter, melted

1 15-ounce can solid-pack pumpkin (not pumpkin-pie mix)

HONEY CREAM

4 tablespoons (½ stick) unsalted butter, at room temperature

4 ounces cream cheese, at room temperature

2 tablespoons honey

½ cup confectioners' sugar

TIP

Make sure you use a can of pure pumpkin, not pumpkin-pie mix.

The honey cream spread for this cake makes it a super-special treat.

1. Preheat oven to 350°F. Butter and lightly flour a 9-by-5-inch loaf pan.

2. In a medium bowl, whisk flour, baking soda, salt and pumpkin-pie spice. In a large bowl, whisk eggs, sugar, melted butter and pumpkin until blended. Fold in dry ingredients just until blended.

3. Pour batter into prepared pan; smooth top. Bake 1 hour, until toothpick inserted in center comes out with just-moist crumbs. Transfer to wire rack; cool in pan 15 minutes. Run a knife around pan edges; invert cake onto rack. Cool completely.

4. For honey cream: In a medium bowl, beat butter, cream cheese, honey and confectioners' sugar until smooth. Serve bread with a pot of honey cream to spread on slices.

Peggy Beldon is an overachiever — she uses the pumpkins from her garden. I use the canned version.

Sugar-Dusted Molasses Crinkles

Serve these old-fashioned favorites with a steaming cup of tea or a tall glass of milk.

1. Preheat oven to 325°F. Line 2 large baking sheets with parchment paper.
2. In a medium bowl, combine flour, salt, baking soda, ginger, cloves and cinnamon.
3. In a large bowl with electric mixer on high speed, beat butter, shortening and both sugars until fluffy. Beat in molasses. Add eggs, 1 at a time, beating well after each addition. Slowly add dry ingredients; beat until combined.
4. Pour about ¼ cup granulated sugar into a small shallow bowl. Scoop up about ¼ cup dough; form a 2-inch ball by rolling dough between your palms. Roll balls in sugar. Repeat with remaining dough. Place on prepared sheets about 3 inches apart. Using a glass, gently press down on balls to flatten slightly.
5. Bake 12 minutes, until puffed and cracked on top. Cookies will still be slightly soft. Transfer to wire rack to cool.

Makes about 32

4½ cups all-purpose flour

½ teaspoon salt

2 teaspoons baking soda

2 teaspoons ground ginger

1 teaspoon ground cloves

1½ teaspoons ground cinnamon

½ cup (1 stick) unsalted butter, at room temperature

½ cup vegetable shortening

1 cup granulated sugar, plus ¼ cup extra for dipping

1 cup brown sugar

½ cup plus 2 tablespoons molasses

2 large eggs

I never expect these to last long, especially if Jack Griffin's visiting.

TIP

Use dark molasses for baking. It has a fuller, less sweet flavor than the light variety. Avoid blackstrap molasses, which is quite bitter.

Broccoli Quiche with Ham and Gruyère

Serves 8

1 refrigerated or frozen pie shell, thawed

1 cup broccoli florets

2 large eggs

2 egg yolks

¾ cup whole milk

¾ cup heavy cream

Salt and pepper, to taste

1 cup diced deli ham (about 4 ounces)

½ cup shredded Gruyère or Jarlsberg cheese

TIP

Prebaking the pie crust prevents it from becoming soggy and tasting raw in the finished quiche.

The center of this quiche will be surprisingly soft when it comes out of the oven, but the filling will continue to set (and sink a bit) as it cools.

1. Partially bake pie shell according to package directions.
2. Preheat oven to 375°F; set oven rack to center position. In a medium saucepan, cook broccoli in boiling water 2 minutes, until tender-crisp. Drain well.
3. In a medium bowl, whisk whole eggs and yolks, milk, cream, salt and pepper until blended.
4. Spread broccoli, ham and cheese evenly over bottom of warm pie shell. Pour in egg mixture to ¼ inch below crust rim (you may have extra, don't fill it up). Bake 35 minutes, until lightly golden brown and a knife blade inserted near the edge comes out clean, and the center feels set but soft. Transfer to wire rack to cool. Serve warm or at room temperature.

I'm here to tell you real men do eat quiche. Just ask Ben.

Asian Peanut Noodle Salad with Chicken and Red Grapes

This is a mild version of the popular restaurant staple. Increase the pepper flakes if you like it spicier.

1. For dressing: In blender or food processor, purée all dressing ingredients until smooth, about 2 minutes. If mixture seems too thick, add hot water, 1 tablespoon at a time, until the consistency of heavy cream.
2. Trim excess fat and skin from chicken. In a medium saucepan, place chicken and water to cover over medium-high heat. Bring to a simmer; poach 10 minutes, or until chicken is just cooked. Remove chicken to cutting board; let rest 5 minutes. Shred chicken into bite-size strips.
3. Meanwhile, cook noodles according to package directions. Drain, then rinse with cold water until cool to touch. In large bowl, toss noodles with chicken, scallions, cucumber and dressing until coated. Gently fold in grapes. Garnish with cilantro, if desired.

TIP

Toss the noodles with the sauce while they are still warm or the noodles will get gloppy.

Serves 4

DRESSING

½ cup smooth peanut butter

¼ cup soy sauce

⅓ cup warm water

2 tablespoons rice-wine vinegar

2 tablespoons toasted sesame oil (see tip on page 110)

2 tablespoons brown sugar

1 tablespoon minced and peeled fresh ginger

2 cloves garlic, chopped

½ teaspoon red-pepper flakes, if desired

SALAD

2 boneless, skinless chicken-breast halves

1 pound Asian rice noodles or 12 ounces spaghetti

3 scallions, thinly sliced

1 cucumber, peeled, seeded and diced

1 cup red grapes, halved

½ cup chopped fresh cilantro, for garnish

Honey-Walnut and Butter Scones

Here's a basic recipe for this classic Scottish quick bread. For variations, add ½ cup shredded cheese or 2 tablespoons chopped fresh thyme or tarragon.

1. Preheat oven to 400°F; set oven rack to middle position. Line a large baking sheet with parchment paper.
2. In food processor, pulse flour, sugar, cream of tartar, baking soda and salt until blended. Add butter pieces; process until mixture resembles coarse meal. Transfer mixture to large bowl.
3. Make a well in the center of mixture; whisk honey into milk and pour milk into well. Stir to form a soft dough. Add walnuts and stir briefly to blend. Turn dough onto a floured countertop. (Dough will be wet.)
4. Using floured hands, press dough into a ½-inch-thick round. Using a sharp knife, cut round into 8 wedges. Gently place wedges on prepared sheet. Bake 15 minutes, until scones are lightly browned around the edges. Transfer to a wire rack to cool.

Makes 8 wedges

2 cups all-purpose flour

1 tablespoon granulated sugar

1 teaspoon cream of tartar

½ teaspoon baking soda

½ teaspoon salt

4 tablespoons (½ stick) cold unsalted butter, diced

2 tablespoons honey

⅔ cup whole milk or half-and-half

½ cup chopped walnuts

TIP

Scones don't keep well. Either eat these the day they are baked, or wrap tightly and freeze.

If you need walnuts, my backyard trees give me an abundant supply every year.

Peanut Butter Sandwich Cookies

*Makes about 30
sandwich cookies*

COOKIE DOUGH

2 cups all-purpose flour

1½ teaspoons baking soda

½ teaspoon salt

1 cup (2 sticks) unsalted butter,
at room temperature

2 cups creamy peanut butter

1 cup brown sugar

1 cup granulated sugar, plus
extra for topping

2 large eggs

2 teaspoons vanilla extract

FILLING

6 ounces cream cheese, at
room temperature

½ cup creamy peanut butter

½ cup confectioners' sugar

TIP

Line the baking sheet with
parchment for even browning
and to guard against burning.

C hewy, crunchy, sweet and salty. What more does anyone need?

1. Preheat oven to 350°F. Line two baking sheets with parchment
   paper.
2. In a medium bowl, combine flour, baking soda and salt. In a large
   bowl with electric mixer at high speed, beat butter, peanut butter
   and both sugars until light and fluffy. Beat in eggs and vanilla.
   Gently fold in flour mixture until just incorporated.
3. Roll a rounded tablespoon of dough between your hands to make
   a ball. Place balls onto prepared sheets. Dip a fork in additional
   granulated sugar; press each dough ball to make crisscross pattern.
   Bake 14 minutes, until lightly brown around the edges. Cool on
   baking sheet 5 minutes. Transfer to wire rack to cool.
4. For filling: Beat all ingredients together until creamy. Spread about
   1 tablespoon filling between 2 cooled cookies.

*I have one word to
describe these cookies.
"Yummy." They'll
disappear faster
than popcorn
at a movie.*

Super Fudge Brownies

Makes 24 brownies

5 large eggs

3½ cups granulated sugar

1 tablespoon vanilla extract

1 cup (2 sticks) unsalted butter

1 8-ounce box unsweetened baking chocolate, coarsely chopped

1 tablespoon instant espresso powder

1¾ cups all-purpose flour

½ teaspoon salt

TIP

Lining the pan with foil makes for easy cleanup. Just lift the entire cooled brownie block out of the pan, then cut into individual brownies.

The only brownie recipe you will ever need. They are the fudgy type of brownie—you won't be able to cut them into squares until they are completely cool. In warm weather, store in the refrigerator.

1. Preheat oven to 375°F. Set rack to upper third of oven. Line a 9-by-13-inch baking pan with a large sheet of foil, pressing foil so that it fits into the pan. Lightly butter foil.

2. In a large bowl with electric mixer on high speed, beat eggs, sugar and vanilla 10 minutes, until blended. Meanwhile, in a glass measuring cup, microwave butter and chocolate until almost melted. Stir in espresso powder until combined.

3. Reduce mixer speed to low; add chocolate mixture until blended. Mix in flour and salt until just combined.

4. Pour batter into prepared pan. Bake 25 minutes, until top is shiny and slightly cracked along the edges. Brownies will still be soft and gooey in the middle. Do not overbake. Transfer to wire rack to cool. When completely cool, use foil edges to lift brownies out of pan. Cover and let sit at least 4 hours before cutting.

*Super Fudge Brownies.
Need I say more!*

Best Blueberry Muffins

akers tip: if using frozen blueberries, do not thaw them before adding to the batter.

1. Preheat oven to 400°F. Line a standard muffin tin with paper liners. In large bowl, combine flour, sugar, baking powder and salt until combined. With pastry blender or two knives, cut in butter until mixture resembles fine crumbs.
2. In a small bowl, whisk egg, milk, lemon zest and vanilla until blended. Fold egg mixture into flour mixture gently, just until flour is moistened (batter will be lumpy). Carefully fold in blueberries.
3. Spoon batter evenly into muffin cups. Bake 20 to 25 minutes until golden and toothpick inserted in center comes out clean. Remove muffins from pan. Transfer to wire rack to cool.

Makes 12 muffins

1¾ cup all-purpose flour

⅔ cup granulated sugar

1 tablespoon baking powder

¾ teaspoon salt

6 tablespoons cold unsalted butter, diced

1 large egg

½ cup plus 2 tablespoons milk

1 teaspoon grated lemon zest

½ teaspoon vanilla extract

1 cup fresh or frozen blueberries

TIP

Remember to fold the wet ingredients into the dry only until moistened. This makes the most tender muffin.

Crumb Bun Muffins

Makes 12 muffins

TOPPING AND FILLING

½ cup granulated sugar

½ cup brown sugar

⅓ cup all-purpose flour

1 tablespoon ground cinnamon

3 tablespoons cold unsalted butter, diced

½ cup chopped pecans

MUFFINS

2 large eggs

1 cup sour cream or plain yogurt

2 teaspoons vanilla extract

1¾ cups all-purpose flour

⅔ cup granulated sugar

1 tablespoon baking powder

Pinch salt

5 tablespoons unsalted butter, at room temperature

TIP

Always cool muffins completely before storing them. If enclosed in an airtight container while still hot, the muffins will get soggy.

These morning treats are just like tiny coffee cakes. They beg for a cup of coffee! They taste best the day they are made.

1. Preheat oven to 375°F. Line a muffin tin with paper liners.
2. For filling: In food processor, combine sugars, flour and cinnamon. Remove ¾ cup of this mixture for the filling. Add butter and pecans to the sugar mixture remaining in the processor; pulse until blended. Transfer this mixture to a bowl for the topping.
3. For muffins: In a medium bowl, whisk eggs, sour cream or yogurt and vanilla until blended. In same food processor (no need to wash), pulse flour, sugar, baking powder and salt until combined. Add egg mixture and butter; pulse until just combined. Do not overmix.
4. Drop a heaping tablespoon of batter into each muffin cup; press batter into cup. Top with about 1 tablespoon filling. Fill cups with remaining batter, then mound streusel over batter. Very lightly press streusel into batter to make it stick.
5. Bake 22 minutes, until a toothpick inserted in center comes out clean. Let muffins cool in pan for 20 minutes. Transfer to wire rack to cool completely.

Jon Bowman says he could eat these all day. Maybe he should. He's much too skinny.

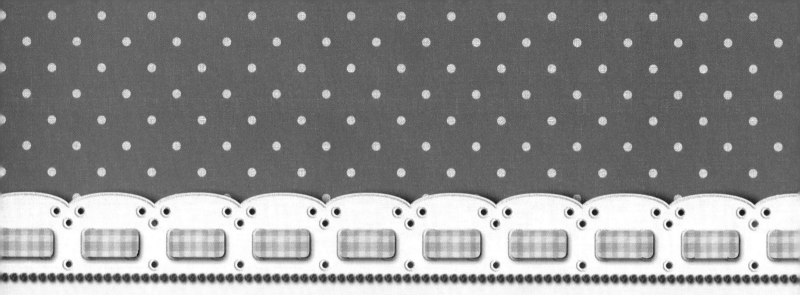

Appetizers

at **311 PELICAN COURT** *with*

Zach and Rosie Cox

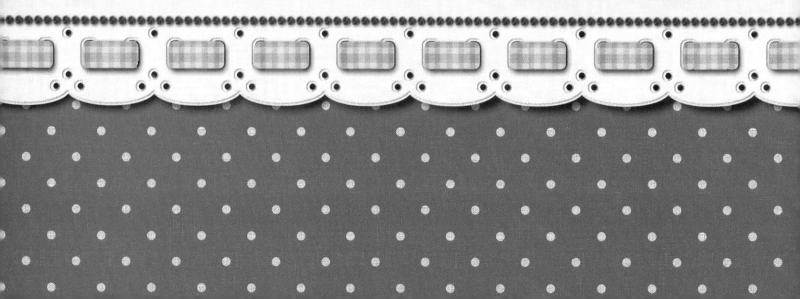

I've known the Cox family for ages. Zach, who's an accountant, has been doing my taxes for close to two decades. He's also involved in community activities, like coaching his son Eddie's soccer team, and being a church deacon.

His wife, Rosie, is a full-time teacher now. She's certainly done her share of volunteer work, back when she was a stay-at-home mom. I served on a couple of committees with her and found her to be the kind of woman who never hesitates to take on a task. I'm afraid that several organizations (which shall remain nameless) took advantage of her willingness to serve. If no one else stepped forward, Rosie did whatever had to be done, and she did it with efficiency and enthusiasm.

Not surprisingly, Rosie is also a skilled cook. Her Shrimp and Cream Cheese Canapés were the talk of the church buffet several years running. Naturally I asked for the recipe and she was kind enough to pass it along. In exchange she asked if I'd share several of my own appetizer recipes, which I was perfectly willing to do. Because she and Zach host an annual cocktail party for his clients, which I've been privileged to attend, Rosie has accumulated a collection of recipes through the years, each of them taste-tested by discerning guests (like *moi*).

One I gave her was for Parmesan Cheese Twists with Fresh Herb Dip. She tried it at a teachers' party and told me everyone raved about it. That didn't surprise me. My friends often tell me how much they enjoy it.

You may have heard that Rosie and Zach got divorced a few years ago. I wasn't privy to what caused the problems in their marriage, but I do know Olivia made quite a controversial ruling during the divorce proceedings.

Rosie and Zach had set up a complicated schedule for shared custody. Allison was in junior high then and Eddie in grade school. According to the parenting plan, those poor kids were going to be shuffled back and forth from one home to the other every few days. All too common a solution, I suppose, but I thought it was ridiculous.

Thankfully Olivia saw the situation the same way I did. She caused quite a stir when she decreed that the kids should stay in the house and the parents should be the ones to move in and out.

I don't know if Olivia had some premonition that Rosie and Zach would fall in love again, but that's exactly what happened. I can tell you everyone was happy to see it, too. Divorce devastates families and while I realize it's often necessary, I just hate to see a family torn apart. But in this case everything worked out beautifully, thanks in no small part to Olivia's wisdom. (I'm her mother, so I'm allowed to brag, don't you think?)

Rosie began working at the elementary school during their separation and after their divorce, but once she and Zach remarried, she decided to continue teaching. She still manages to do some volunteering. At the moment she's working with Grace at the library to start an interesting program, in which children read to dogs. When I first heard that, I was sure something was wrong with my hearing. Dogs in the library? But after Rosie told me about it—how dogs make the kids feel comfortable because they don't *judge* their reading ability—I felt it was very sensible. Dogs and kids belong together, don't they? I remember when…

No, wait, I'm digressing. I find I do that more often now that I'm getting on in years. But I believe we're as young or as old as we make up our minds to be. Before I get sidetracked again I want to mention some of my favorite appetizers and urge you to try the Roasted Red Pepper, Goat Cheese and Tarragon Pinwheels. They're delicious and nutritious, too.

In fact, my husband, Ben, recently read an article on how good red peppers are for one's health. All that Vitamin C, you know. So I made this for him the very next day, and he's been asking for them ever since.

Turn these pages for appetizer recipes guaranteed to make your next party an unqualified success!

Eggplant Caponata with Toasted Pita Crisps

Makes 5 cups caponata and 36 crisps

CAPONATA

4 tablespoons olive oil, divided, plus extra for brushing

1 medium eggplant, cut into small cubes

2 bell peppers, any color, cut into cubes

1 small onion, finely chopped

1 stalk celery, thinly sliced

1 15-ounce can diced tomatoes

¾ cup tomato juice or V8

2 tablespoons red-wine vinegar

2 tablespoons brown sugar

1 tablespoon drained capers

Salt and pepper, to taste

PITA CRISPS

3 pita pockets

Olive oil

Kosher or sea salt

This classic Sicilian relish is endlessly adaptable. Use it as a sauce for pasta, a topping for grilled meat or fish, or a sandwich spread.

1. Warm 2 tablespoons of the oil in a large skillet over medium heat. Add eggplant; cook 8 minutes, until softened and lightly browned, stirring often. Transfer eggplant to bowl. Add remaining oil to skillet, still over medium heat. Cook bell peppers, onion and celery 8 minutes, stirring often.

2. Add eggplant, diced tomatoes and tomato juice to skillet. Cover and cook 15 minutes, until vegetables are soft and flavors are combined, stirring often. Stir in vinegar, sugar and capers; warm through. Season to taste with salt and pepper. Serve warm or at room temperature.

3. For pita crisps: Preheat oven to 350°F. Cut pita rounds into 6 wedges; separate wedges to create 36 wedges. Arrange wedges, rough-side up, in a single layer on two large baking sheets; brush with oil. Sprinkle with kosher or sea salt. Bake 12 minutes, until crisp and golden. Transfer to wire rack to cool.

> **TIP**
>
> Both the relish and the crisps can be made up to 3 days in advance. Store in airtight containers—the caponata in refrigerator, the crisps at room temperature.

Shown on page 5

Shrimp and Cream Cheese Canapés

The shrimp spread can be prepared 2 days in advance, making this elegant appetizer easy to throw together at the last minute.

1. Preheat oven to 300°F. Slice baguette on the diagonal into very thin (about ¼-inch) slices. Arrange slices on a large baking sheet. Lightly brush 1 side of each slice with oil. Bake 12 minutes, until lightly toasted. Transfer to wire rack to cool.

2. Melt 1 tablespoon of the butter in a medium skillet over medium heat. Add shallot; cook 2 minutes, until softened, stirring often. Add shrimp, salt and pepper; cook 3 minutes, until shrimp are pink and cooked through, stirring often. Add sherry; cook until almost all liquid is evaporated. Transfer mixture to a food processor. Add cream cheese, lemon juice and remaining 2 tablespoons butter; pulse 5 times until coarsely chopped but not puréed. Season with salt and pepper. Refrigerate until ready to use.

3. Spread shrimp mixture on crostini. Garnish with parsley. Serve cool or at room temperature.

Ever since Ruth got dentures, these are her favorite appetizers.

Makes about 40

1 French baguette

Olive oil

3 tablespoons unsalted butter, at room temperature, divided

1 medium shallot, finely chopped

½ pound shrimp, shelled and deveined

Salt and pepper, to taste

3 tablespoons medium-dry sherry

3 ounces cream cheese, at room temperature

2 tablespoons fresh lemon juice

Fresh parsley, sprigs or chopped, for garnish

TIP

Toast the bread up to 4 days in advance. Store, tightly covered, at room temperature.

Parmesan Cheese Twists with Fresh Herb Dip

After you first try this recipe, you may find that one batch of these crispy twists is not nearly enough.

1. Preheat oven to 400°F. Line a large baking sheet with parchment paper.
2. On lightly floured countertop, roll out pastry to a 10-by-14-inch rectangle. Cut in half lengthwise; brush both halves with egg yolk mixture. Top one of the halves with Parmesan, salt and paprika. Place the other half onto the Parmesan-topped half, coated sides together. Press down on rectangle to seal the two pieces. Sprinkle with additional salt. Using a sharp knife, cut crosswise into 24 slices, each about ½-inch thick.
3. Pick up one strip, holding an end in each hand. Twist ends in opposite directions. Lay twisted strips on prepared sheet. Bake 10 minutes, until golden and crisp. Transfer to wire racks to cool.
4. For dip: In blender or food processor, process parsley, basil, chives, lemon juice and cream cheese until blended. Add yogurt and oil; blend until combined. Season to taste with salt and pepper. Cover and refrigerate until serving.

TIP

It's the fresh herbs and lemon juice that make this dip sing—dried herbs won't do the trick.

Makes 24 twists and 1 cup dip

TWISTS

1 sheet (7 ounces) frozen puff pastry, thawed

1 egg yolk beaten with 1 tablespoon water

6 tablespoons grated Parmesan cheese, divided

Salt

Paprika

DIP

½ cup chopped fresh parsley

¼ cup chopped fresh basil

2 tablespoons chopped fresh chives

2 tablespoons fresh lemon juice

3 ounces cream cheese, at room temperature

½ cup plain yogurt

1 tablespoon olive oil

Salt and pepper, to taste

Ginger Chicken Skewers with Peanut Dipping Sauce

Makes about 25 skewers and about 1¾ cups sauce

CHICKEN

¼ cup soy sauce

2 tablespoons fresh lime juice

1 tablespoon honey

1 tablespoon minced fresh ginger

1 tablespoon brown sugar

1 clove garlic, minced

1½ pounds boneless, skinless chicken breasts or thighs, trimmed and cut into ½-inch strips

PEANUT DIPPING SAUCE

¾ cup peanut butter

¾ cup unsweetened coconut milk, plus extra if needed

¼ cup brown sugar

2 tablespoons fresh lime juice

2 tablespoons soy sauce

2 tablespoons minced fresh ginger

Dash hot sauce

This recipe yields plenty of creamy sauce. Toss leftover sauce with noodles and cucumber strips for a quick weeknight dinner. Add hot-pepper flakes if your family likes it spicy.

1. For chicken: In a large bowl, combine first six ingredients, stirring until sugar dissolves. Add chicken strips to bowl; marinate at least 30 minutes, turning chicken occasionally to coat.

2. Preheat grill or grill pan to medium-high. Thread each chicken piece lengthwise onto a skewer, keeping strip as flat as possible. Discard marinade.

3. Grill skewers about 5 minutes, turning often.

4. For sauce: In blender or food processor, blend all ingredients until combined. Pour in additional coconut milk until sauce is the consistency of heavy cream. Serve skewers with sauce on the side for dipping.

> **TIP**
>
> Soak the wooden skewers in water for 30 minutes before threading the chicken strips. This will guard against burning.

Roasted Red Pepper, Goat Cheese and Tarragon Pinwheels

(A)lmost any fresh herb will work with this savory blend of roasted pepper and creamy cheese.

1. Preheat broiler. Line a baking sheet with foil. Halve pepper, then core and seed. Press pepper flat, skin-side up, on prepared pan. Broil 10 minutes, until skins are blackened. Transfer to a bowl and cover with foil (use the same foil that lined the pan). Let stand 20 minutes. Peel pepper and discard blackened skin; thinly slice the roasted pepper.

2. Warm a dry, heavy skillet over medium heat. Place 1 tortilla in pan. Cook until warm and lightly speckled brown, about 10 seconds. Remove from pan; cover with a dish towel. Repeat with remaining tortillas.

3. Spread a warm tortilla with 2 tablespoons goat cheese. Top with about ¼ of the pepper strips. Sprinkle with some tarragon and salt. Roll up tortilla gently but firmly. Wrap securely in plastic wrap. Repeat with remaining tortillas and filling ingredients. Refrigerate at least 1 hour (but no longer than 4 hours).

4. Unwrap tortillas; slice off ragged ends. Cut each wrap diagonally into 5 slices. Arrange on platter; serve chilled or at room temperature.

Makes about 20

1 red bell pepper

4 medium flour tortillas

½ cup spreadable goat cheese (like Chavrie)

½ cup chopped fresh tarragon, basil or mint

Salt, to taste

TIP

Warming the tortillas before filling them prevents them from becoming gummy.

The marinated red peppers that come in a jar work well, too. Only don't tell Ben that.

Mini-Hamburgers with the Works

Makes 20 hamburgers

¾ pound ground chuck

1 tablespoon Worcestershire sauce

½ teaspoon onion powder

½ teaspoon garlic powder

Salt and pepper, to taste

5 hamburger buns or rolls, split and lightly toasted

Garnishes: Ketchup, sliced cornichons or small pickle, lettuce leaves

TIP

These are best served warm, but you can form the patties and cut the buns in advance.

Either assemble these mini-bites for your guests, or set out the garnishes and let them top their own burgers.

1. In a large bowl, combine beef, Worcestershire, onion powder, garlic powder, salt and pepper. Divide mixture into 20 walnut-sized pieces. Using wet hands, roll pieces into balls; flatten into patties.

2. Preheat grill or grill pan over medium-high heat. Cook patties 3 minutes per side, until cooked through.

3. Meanwhile, cut each bun into 4 rounds with a 1½-inch biscuit cutter, creating 20 bottoms and 20 tops. Place burgers on bottom buns; top with garnishes as desired. Gently press on top bun.

My short friend Bess says these are the perfect size for her.

Caramelized Onion Tart with Black Olives

Serves 16

3 tablespoons olive oil, plus extra for pan

Cornmeal or flour, for pan

1 ball prepared pizza dough (about 1 pound)

3 large onions (about 1½ pounds), very thinly sliced

Salt and pepper, to taste

1 teaspoon chopped fresh thyme or ½ teaspoon dried

10 black olives, such as Nicoise, pitted and coarsely chopped

TIP

To pit olives, hit them with the flat side of a knife to break the flesh, remove the pit and set the olive pieces aside to garnish the tart.

You can find pizza dough in the supermarket's refrigerated or freezer aisle, or you can buy it from your local pizza parlor—most will sell you an unbaked ball of dough. No matter where you buy it, pizza dough varies in composition, which affects baking time. Keep an eye on your tart so that it doesn't burn.

1. Preheat oven to 425°F. Brush a large baking sheet with oil; sprinkle with flour or cornmeal. Roll out dough on a lightly floured counter to a 10-by-14-inch rectangle. Transfer to prepared sheet; let dough rest 30 minutes while you cook the onions.

2. Warm 3 tablespoons oil in a large skillet over low heat. Add onions, salt and pepper. Cook 30 minutes, stirring often, until onions turn light golden but not brown. Remove from heat; stir in thyme.

3. Spread onions evenly over dough; dot with olives. Bake 13 minutes, until crisp and hot. Serve warm or at room temperature.

Some of my best recipes come from wakes. I got this at Wally Porter's. Such a dear man.

Smoked Salmon Canapés with Horseradish Cream

If you're not using cocktail bread, use a 2-inch fluted round or other pastry cutter to cut slices of normal-sized bread into party-ready decorative shapes.

1. Cut smoked salmon into 20 one-inch strips.
2. In a small bowl, combine sour cream and horseradish until blended. Spread evenly on bread rounds. Curl salmon slices on top of cream like a ribbon; garnish with a grind of pepper, a dill sprig and a few capers. Serve cool or at room temperature.

Makes about 20

4 ounces smoked salmon slices

½ cup sour cream

1 tablespoon prepared horseradish, or to taste

21 pieces pumpernickel "cocktail bread," or 7 very thin slices pumpernickel or whole-grain bread

Garnishes: Freshly ground pepper, fresh dill sprigs, drained capers

TIP

It's easier to separate the salmon slices when cold.

Celery Cups with Blue Cheese Mousse and Bacon

A dinner fork is the best tool for blending the crumbly blue cheese with the cream cheese.

1. Cook bacon until crisp. Transfer to paper-towel-lined plate. Chop or break into triangular pieces.
2. In a medium bowl, beat blue and cream cheese until combined and mostly smooth. Season with salt and pepper.
3. Cut each celery stalk on the diagonal into five pieces. Using a small spoon, smooth about 1 teaspoon of cheese mixture along each celery cup. Set a few shards of bacon into the cheese mixture in each cup. Sprinkle with chives.

Makes about 20

6 slices bacon

3 ounces blue cheese, at room temperature

3 ounces cream cheese, at room temperature

Salt and pepper, to taste

4 stalks celery

Fresh chives, snipped, for garnish

TIP

Be sure to use block cream cheese, not the whipped kind.

I brought these to the senior potluck once and they disappeared so fast I didn't even get one.

Dinner

at 44 CRANBERRY POINT *with*

Bob and Peggy Beldon

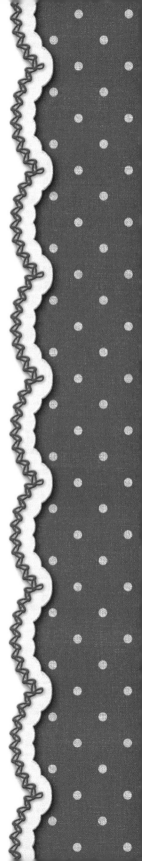

I knew Bob and Peggy as high school sweethearts back when Peggy hung around with Olivia and Grace. Bob was a good friend of Dan Sherman's, too, as I recall. They were on the football team and enlisted in the army together, leaving for Vietnam shortly after graduation.

Bob and Peggy were married after he returned from the war and they lived in Spokane for quite a few years. Every once in a while, I'd run into Bob's mother, who'd tell me how they were doing, but Aggie died in the late '90s. I heard nothing more about Bob and Peggy until the summer of 2002, when they moved back to Cedar Cove to retire. They bought the old Crockett property, which was a dilapidated, abandoned wreck of a place, a real eyesore out there on Cranberry Point.

When Bob and Peggy made an offer on it, the rumor was that they intended to turn it into a bed-and-breakfast. Well, the rumor was right, but I don't mind telling you I was one of the skeptics. To my way of thinking, it would've been better to tear down that ramshackle old dump and build something new.

Bob proved me wrong. He must've worked night and day for six months. Some retirement! He told me he wasn't interested in sitting around watching the grass grow, but I had no idea he'd turned into such a handyman. With only occasional hired help, he gutted the house, replaced walls and windows, re-roofed and painted the exterior. Peggy did a lot of the interior painting and refinished the furniture they'd bought in junk stores. Not only that, she created the most beautiful gardens. All in all, the results are spectacular, and I'm not the only person who thinks so. They've been written up in some fancy travel magazines, too.

The day Bob and Peggy hung up their sign for Thyme and Tide Bed & Breakfast, they held an open house for the community. Peggy served a Roasted Garlic White Pizza that was to die for. (I like that expression, although my granddaughter tells me it's out-of-date.) Peggy shared that recipe and the one for Fresh Herb Crab Cakes—the best I've ever tasted.

I confess that when I first saw Peggy's herb garden I was struck with envy; if the expression "green thumb" applies to anyone, it does to Peggy. As you've already guessed, she's a wonder in the kitchen, too. And perhaps most important of all, Peggy has the gift of hospitality. Everyone who stops in is immediately welcomed and served a cup of tea and the most delectable baked treats.

Even though the B and B is a major success, the Beldons haven't always had an easy time of it. A great deal of unpleasant speculation fell on them when one of their overnight guests died under suspicious circumstances. Some people actually had the nerve to suggest Bob was responsible! Fortunately the case was eventually solved by Sheriff Davis, with the assistance of Roy McAfee, our local P.I., and since then Thyme and Tide has done a steady business with plenty of repeat customers.

The breakfasts Peggy provides at Thyme and Tide are legendary. But here's a little-known fact—her dinners are just as good. Possibly even better. Luckily Bob keeps fit working around the yard and maintaining the house, otherwise he'd be a serious candidate for a weight-loss program. Peggy's Seared Scallops with Mushroom Ragout are so good that if nobody was looking, you'd lick your plate. And her Shrimp Enchiladas—the only word that comes to mind is *incomparable*. I know she got her wonderful Macaroni and Cheese recipe from Teri Polgar. It's the ultimate comfort food.

Do take time to browse through these recipes and if you ever have the opportunity to dine at 44 Cranberry Point, count yourself fortunate.

Lasagna Bolognese for a Crowd

Serves 10

1 tablespoon olive oil

1 medium onion, chopped

2 medium carrots, thinly sliced

4 cloves garlic, minced

8 ounces lean ground beef

8 ounces spicy Italian sausage, casings removed

8 ounces sweet sausage, casings removed

Salt and pepper, to taste

1 28-ounce can crushed tomatoes with purée

1 15-ounce can diced tomatoes

1 6-ounce can tomato paste

2 tablespoons brown sugar

2 tablespoons dried oregano

1 bay leaf

15 lasagna noodles (about 12 ounces)

2 15-ounce containers part-skim ricotta cheese

1 cup grated Parmesan cheese

2 large eggs

5 cups shredded mozzarella cheese (about 1¼ pounds)

This hearty lasagna is a great make-ahead dish—it tastes even better the next day. For even longer storage, wrap tightly and freeze in anticipation of a day when you don't have time to cook.

1. Warm oil in a large saucepan or Dutch oven over medium-low heat. Add onion and carrots; cook 6 minutes, until softened, stirring often. Stir in garlic; cook 1 minute. Add beef, both sausages, salt and pepper; cook 8 minutes, stirring and using a wooden spoon to break up meat. Add crushed and diced tomatoes, tomato paste, sugar, oregano and bay leaf. Cover; bring to a simmer. Simmer 20 minutes, stirring occasionally. Remove bay leaf.

2. Meanwhile, cook noodles according to package directions. Drain. In a large bowl, combine noodles and cold water to cover.

3. In a medium bowl, whisk ricotta, Parmesan and eggs until blended. Season with salt and pepper.

4. Preheat oven to 350°F. Spread ½ cup of the meat sauce in bottom of a deep 9-by-13-inch glass baking dish. Remove noodles from water; lay 5 noodles on top of sauce, overlapping noodles. Spread half of the ricotta mixture over noodles; sprinkle 2 cups of mozzarella over ricotta. Spread 2½ cups of meat sauce over mozzarella. Layer 5 more noodles, remaining ricotta, 2 cups mozzarella, and 2½ cups meat sauce. Finish with 5 remaining noodles, remaining meat sauce, and remaining 1 cup mozzarella. Cover pan with foil. Bake 40 minutes. Remove foil and bake 30 minutes, until bubbling. Let sit 10 minutes before serving.

TIP

For best flavor, grate fresh Parmesan and mozzarella, rather than using preshredded cheese.

Seared Scallops with Mushroom Ragout

Since scallops cook so quickly, it's important to preheat the pan before you add the fish; this allows the outside to get nice and brown before the inside gets overcooked and tough.

1. Pat scallops dry with paper towel; season with salt and pepper and sprinkle with flour.
2. Warm oil in a large heavy skillet over medium-high heat until hot but not smoking. Cook scallops 4 minutes per side, until golden-brown and just cooked through. Transfer to a platter and loosely cover with foil.
3. Melt 3 tablespoons of the butter in same skillet over medium-high heat. Add mushrooms; cook 4 minutes, until golden, stirring occasionally. Add shallots; cook 1 minute, stirring. Add sherry and vinegar; simmer 2 minutes, stirring occasionally. Remove from heat; stir in remaining 1 tablespoon butter. Spoon sauce over scallops.

Serves 4

1½ pounds large sea scallops (about 20), tough ligament removed if attached

Salt and pepper, to taste

Flour for dredging

2 tablespoons olive oil

4 tablespoons (½ stick) unsalted butter, divided

1 pound white or cremini mushrooms, stemmed and quartered

2 medium shallots, chopped

½ cup medium-dry sherry

1 tablespoon balsamic vinegar

Peggy tells me this is Bob's favorite dinner. After trying it I can see why.

TIP

Drying the scallops well with a paper towel before cooking also helps them brown better.

Bowtie Pasta with White Beans, Roasted Peppers and Garlic Spinach

Serves 4

3 red, yellow or orange bell peppers

12 ounces bowtie pasta or penne pasta

1 tablespoon olive oil

4 cloves garlic, minced

1 15-ounce can white beans, rinsed and drained

Salt and pepper, to taste

1 9-ounce bag baby spinach

1 tablespoon balsamic vinegar

½ cup grated Parmesan cheese

TIP

You can roast the peppers up to three days ahead. Drizzle with a little olive oil and store, tightly covered, in the refrigerator.

Don't be alarmed by the amount of spinach you add to the simmering skillet—it cooks down tremendously. Just keep stirring, smashing the beans as you do so, and in minutes you'll have a colorful, flavorful, healthful dish.

1. Preheat broiler. Line a baking sheet with foil. Halve bell peppers, then core and seed. Press peppers flat, skin-side up, onto prepared pan. Broil 10 minutes, until skins are blackened. Transfer to a bowl and cover with foil (use the same foil that lined the pan). Let stand 20 minutes. Peel and discard charred skin from peppers. Thinly slice peppers.

2. Cook pasta according to package directions. Reserve 1 cup cooking water; drain pasta.

3. Warm oil in a large nonstick skillet over medium-low heat. Add garlic; cook 1 minute, stirring often. Add bell peppers, beans, salt and pepper and cook 3 minutes, stirring often. Add pasta cooking water and about ¼ of the spinach; bring to a simmer. Let cook 10 minutes, slowly adding remaining spinach, stirring often and smashing beans against the side of the pan to create a sauce. Remove from heat; stir in vinegar.

4. In a large serving bowl, toss pasta with sauce and Parmesan. Season with salt and pepper.

Casual Chicken Cordon Bleu

Serves 4

4 chicken cutlets or thin-sliced chicken breasts

Salt and pepper, to taste

2 tablespoons unsalted butter

12 baby spinach leaves (about ½ cup)

4 thin slices deli ham (about 2 ounces)

1 cup shredded Gruyère or Jarlsberg cheese

TIP

Smaller, more delicate baby spinach leaves work best in this recipe. If unavailable, use the regular large-leaf variety, first stripping off and discarding the thick stems.

Forget the rolling and the breading usually found in Cordon Bleu recipes. Enjoy the savory chicken, ham-and-cheese-flavor combo in this super-simple weeknight dinner.

1. Pat chicken dry with paper towels; season with salt and pepper. Melt butter in a large heavy skillet over medium heat.

2. Add chicken to pan; increase heat to medium-high and cook 3 minutes, until golden. Flip chicken, top each cutlet with about 3 spinach leaves, 1 slice ham (folding it to fit), and ¼ cup cheese. Cover pan and cook about 3 minutes longer, until chicken is cooked through and cheese is melted.

I let company think this is a lot of work. You can fool them, too.

Chicken Pot Pie

A 2-quart casserole is the perfect dish size here—the crust should hang over the edge, to keep the filling from bubbling over.

1. Warm oil in a large, heavy ovenproof skillet over medium heat. Season chicken with salt and pepper. Cook chicken 6 minutes on each side, until browned. (Chicken will not be cooked through.)

2. Preheat oven to 350°F. In the fat remaining in the skillet, cook carrots, celery, onion, thyme, salt and pepper over medium-low heat for 6 minutes, stirring often, until softened. Increase heat to medium-high. Nestle chicken on top of vegetables, meat-side down. Add broth and any juices from chicken platter and bring to simmer. Place in oven; roast 25 minutes, until chicken is cooked through. Return chicken to plate. Let cool, then remove skin and bones and break meat into 1-inch chunks and shreds.

3. Increase oven temperature to 400°F. Pour contents of skillet through strainer set over a bowl. Transfer vegetables from strainer to a bowl. Reserve broth; you should have about 3½ cups (if not, make up the difference with more broth, water or milk).

4. For sauce: Melt butter in the skillet over medium-high heat. Sprinkle in flour and cook, stirring constantly, until incorporated, about 1 minute. Slowly whisk in 3½ cups reserved broth and milk and bring to boil; reduce heat to medium and simmer about 10 minutes, stirring almost constantly, until sauce is thickened and coats back of spoon. Remove from heat. Stir in shredded chicken, cooked vegetables, peas, parsley, salt and pepper. Pour filling into 2-quart casserole dish. Lay pie crust on top of filling, crimping edges with your fingers. (You may need to roll it on a lightly floured surface to get it to fit your dish.) The crust should hang over the edges of the dish. Slash a few holes in the crust.

5. Bake 30 minutes, until crust is golden and filling bubbles. Let sit 10 minutes before serving.

Serves 6

FILLING

1 tablespoon vegetable oil

4 bone-in, skin-on, chicken breasts

Salt and pepper, to taste

4 carrots, peeled and diced

2 stalks celery, diced

½ medium onion, chopped

1 tablespoon chopped fresh thyme or 1 teaspoon dried whole thyme

4 cups reduced-sodium chicken broth

SAUCE AND CRUST

4 tablespoons (½ stick) unsalted butter

½ cup all-purpose flour

½ cup whole milk

¾ cup frozen peas

¼ cup chopped fresh parsley

1 refrigerated or frozen pie crust, thawed

TIP

For a shiny golden crust, brush the top with beaten egg before baking.

Fresh Herb Crab Cakes with Homemade Tartar Sauce

Lump crabmeat is now available in most supermarkets, making it easier than ever to make this special dish.

1. In a large bowl, combine crab, scallions, breadcrumbs, mayonnaise, parsley, tarragon, chives, salt and pepper. Fold in beaten egg until moistened. Using about ½ cup for each, form mixture into eight 1-inch-thick patties. Place patties on a platter or baking sheet; cover with plastic wrap and refrigerate at least 30 minutes or up to 24 hours.
2. Warm oil in a large nonstick skillet over medium-high heat. Cook cakes 4 minutes per side, or until golden brown and cooked through.
3. For sauce: In a medium bowl, combine all sauce ingredients. Serve with warm crab cakes.

Corrie McAfee passed this on to Peggy and me. The best crab cakes I've ever tasted.

Serves 4

CRAB CAKES

1 pound lump crabmeat, picked over

4 scallions, thinly sliced

¼ cup breadcrumbs

¼ cup mayonnaise

3 tablespoons minced fresh parsley

2 tablespoons minced fresh tarragon

1 tablespoon minced fresh chives

Salt and pepper, to taste

1 large egg, lightly beaten

TARTAR SAUCE

½ cup mayonnaise

2 tablespoons minced cornichons

1 teaspoon cornichon juice

1 tablespoon minced red onion

1 tablespoon minced drained capers

1 tablespoon fresh lemon juice

TIP

Crab cakes hold together better if refrigerated at least 30 minutes before cooking.

Beef Stew with Red Wine

Serves 6

3½ pounds beef stew meat, cut into 1½-inch cubes

Salt and pepper, to taste

3 tablespoons all-purpose flour

5 tablespoons vegetable or light olive oil

1¼ cups dry red wine, divided

1 large onion, chopped

1 14½-ounce can reduced-sodium beef broth

1 28-ounce can whole plum tomatoes

2 teaspoons chopped fresh thyme or 1 teaspoon dried thyme

1 bay leaf

5 carrots, peeled and coarsely chopped

1 10-ounce package white button mushrooms, stemmed and quartered

1 cup water

Serve this family favorite over mashed potatoes or egg noodles.

1. Using paper towel, blot beef dry. In large bowl, toss beef with salt, pepper and flour.
2. Warm 2 tablespoons of the oil in a large pot or Dutch oven over medium-high heat. Add meat in a single layer; cook 6 minutes, turning to brown on all sides. Remove from pot and transfer to a bowl. Add ½ cup of the wine to pot and stir with a wooden spoon, scraping up loose bits on the bottom of the pot. Wine will thicken and combine with pot bits to make a thick sauce. Lift pot off heat and scrape this sauce onto the browned beef. Return pot to heat; add 2 tablespoons oil. Brown remaining beef as above and transfer to bowl. Add another ½ cup wine; deglaze* pot as above and transfer to browned beef.
3. Warm remaining 1 tablespoon oil in same pot over medium heat. Add onion; cook 5 minutes, until softened, stirring often. Add remaining ¼ cup wine, stirring until wine boils off. Return beef and juices in bowl to pot. Add broth, tomatoes, thyme and bay leaf. Bring to a simmer; reduce heat to low, cover and cook for 1½ hours, stirring occasionally and adding water to desired consistency.
4. Stir in carrots, mushrooms and 1 cup water; cover and cook 1 hour, until meat and vegetables are tender. Do not let stew boil; keep at a low simmer. Season with salt and pepper.

TIP

The key to rich beef flavor is *deglazing the pan using wine. This process scrapes up all the browned bits left from cooking the beef and incorporates them into the sauce. The alcohol is cooked off in this process.

Thick Pork Chops with Apple Stuffing and Cider Gravy

For the most succulent chops, select cuts that are at least 1-inch thick.

Serves 4

1. Preheat oven to 425°F; set an oven rack in lower third position. Place a roasting pan or rimmed baking sheet in oven to warm.

2. Warm 1 tablespoon of the oil in a large heavy skillet over medium heat. Add onion and celery; cook 5 minutes, until softened, stirring. Stir in apple, ¼ cup of the cider, thyme, salt and pepper. Cook 4 minutes, stirring occasionally. Remove from the heat; fold in bread cubes and parsley.

3. Using a paring knife, cut a 2-inch-wide pocket into the fatty side of each chop, cutting almost to the bone. Spoon a quarter of the stuffing into each pocket. Using your fingers, pinch the seal together. Season the chops with salt and pepper.

4. Warm the remaining 3 tablespoons oil in same skillet over medium-high heat until shimmering. Add the chops and cook for 3 minutes on each side, until browned. Transfer chops to the preheated roasting pan; set aside the skillet with the cooking fat in it. Roast the chops 15 minutes, flipping them halfway through cooking. Cook until an instant-read thermometer inserted into the stuffing registers 140°F. Transfer the chops to a serving platter and set the roasting pan aside. Tent chops loosely with foil to keep warm.

5. Meanwhile, set reserved skillet over low heat. Sprinkle flour into fat in skillet, stirring until incorporated. Gradually pour in remaining 1 cup cider, stirring constantly and allowing liquid to incorporate before adding additional cider. Bring to a boil; lower the heat and simmer 5 minutes, until liquid reduces to about ¾ cup, whisking occasionally. Scrape any browned bits and juices from the roasting pan into the simmering gravy. Remove skillet from heat; whisk in butter. Season with salt and pepper and spoon sauce over pork chops.

4 tablespoons olive oil, divided

½ small onion, chopped

1 celery stalk, chopped

1 small apple, peeled and diced

1¼ cups apple cider, divided

½ teaspoon chopped fresh thyme

Salt and pepper, to taste

½ cup small bread cubes (from 2 slices)

2 tablespoons chopped fresh parsley

4 bone-in pork chops, 1 inch thick (about 10 ounces each)

1 tablespoon all-purpose flour

1 tablespoon unsalted butter

TIP

Use a small, sharp knife to carve out the pocket for your stuffing. If pocket doesn't stay closed, hold it together with a toothpick.

Roasted Salmon with Creamy Dill Sauce

Serves 4

MUSTARD GLAZE

4 teaspoons olive oil, divided

1 tablespoon Dijon mustard

1 tablespoon fresh lemon juice

Salt and pepper, to taste

4 salmon fillets, about 5 ounces each, with skin

DILL SAUCE

½ cup mayonnaise

½ cup sour cream

1 tablespoon fresh lemon juice

1 scallion, thinly sliced

½ cup finely chopped fresh dill

Salt and pepper, to taste

TIP

Overcooked salmon can be dry. Follow the timing carefully for cooking the fish to keep it moist.

The flavor of wild salmon is preferable to that of farm-raised salmon, but it's expensive and not always available. This recipe will work with either type.

1. Preheat oven to 425°F. Place a large ovenproof skillet over medium-high heat; warm pan 2 minutes. Swirl 3 teaspoons oil into pan.
2. In a small bowl, combine remaining oil, mustard and lemon juice. Season salmon with salt and pepper; place in hot pan, skin-side up. Cook 2 minutes. Turn fish; spoon mustard glaze over top of filets. Place skillet in oven and roast 8 minutes, until golden brown on the outside but no longer red on the inside. Fillet should feel semifirm, not squishy, when poked.
3. For sauce: In a small bowl, combine mayonnaise, sour cream, lemon juice, scallion and dill. Season with salt and pepper. Serve sauce with warm fish.

With wild salmon so plentiful in the Pacific Northwest, this has long been a family specialty.

Ginger Flank Steak and Oyster Sauce Stir-Fry

Serves 4

1¼ pounds flank steak, very thinly sliced

¼ cup reduced-sodium soy sauce

¼ cup oyster sauce

1 tablespoon rice-wine vinegar

1 tablespoon brown sugar

2 teaspoons toasted* (Asian) sesame oil

2 tablespoons water, plus ⅓ cup water

1 teaspoon cornstarch

2 tablespoons peanut or sesame oil, divided

1½ pounds broccoli, cut into small florets and stems thinly sliced

2 red bell peppers, thinly sliced

5 cloves garlic, minced

1 tablespoon ginger, minced and peeled (from a 1-inch piece)

2 scallions, thinly sliced

Serve this better-than-take-out stir-fry over rice. For best flavor and quickest cooking, the beef and peppers should be sliced very thin.

1. In a medium bowl, combine beef slices and soy sauce. Marinate beef at least 30 minutes or up to 2 hours. In a small cup, whisk oyster sauce, vinegar, sugar, dark sesame oil and 2 tablespoons water. Whisk in cornstarch to form a thick paste.

2. Warm 1 tablespoon peanut oil in a large nonstick skillet or wok over high heat. Add beef and cook about 2 minutes, stirring often. Beef will be browned but not cooked through. Transfer beef to a large bowl.

3. Warm same skillet over medium heat. Add broccoli and cook 1 minute, stirring. Add ⅓ cup water, cover pan and cook 2 minutes, until broccoli is tender-crisp. Transfer to plate with beef.

4. Warm remaining 1 tablespoon peanut oil in same skillet over medium heat. Add pepper strips and cook 2 minutes, stirring. Add garlic and ginger and cook 30 seconds, until fragrant, stirring constantly. Return beef, broccoli and any juices in the bowl to skillet. Add oyster sauce mixture and cook 1 minute, stirring constantly, until sauce thickens and beef and vegetables are coated. Transfer to platter and serve over rice. Garnish with scallions.

TIP

*There are two different types of sesame oil. Toasted, sometimes called Asian or dark, sesame oil is intensely flavored and is used sparingly in sauces. Regular sesame oil is lightly flavored and is used as a cooking oil.

Fettuccine Alfredo with Garlic Shrimp and Scallops

Since shrimp and scallops cook so quickly, this is one of those sauces that you can complete in the time it takes to cook the pasta.

1. Warm oil in a large heavy saucepan over medium heat. Add garlic; cook 30 seconds, stirring. Pat scallops dry with paper towel. Add shrimp, scallops, salt and pepper to skillet and cook 5 minutes, stirring often. Remove from heat.
2. Cook pasta according to package directions. Reserve ¼ cup cooking water; drain pasta.
3. Melt butter in a large saucepan over low heat. Add cooked pasta; toss with butter to coat. Stir in cheese, reserved cooking water, half-and-half, salt and pepper. Using tongs, transfer pasta to four serving plates. Pile shrimp and scallops atop pasta; garnish with parsley.

Serves 4

2 tablespoons olive oil

5 garlic cloves, minced

8 ounces bay scallops

8 ounces fresh or frozen peeled and deveined large shrimp, thawed

Salt and pepper, to taste

12 ounces fettuccine or spaghetti

6 tablespoons unsalted butter

1 cup grated Parmesan cheese, plus more for sprinkling

½ cup half-and-half

½ cup chopped fresh parsley, for garnish

Grace Harding served this and I refused to leave the house until she handed over the recipe.

TIP

There are two varieties of scallops. This recipe calls for the smaller, sweeter bay scallops. You can substitute larger sea scallops, but be sure to cook them a few minutes longer.

Chili Pie with Cheddar Hash Brown Topping

This casserole is a great make-ahead dish. Just wrap the entire casserole in plastic and foil and freeze for up to a month. Thaw overnight in the refrigerator, then bring to room temperature before topping with the potatoes and baking.

1. Preheat oven to 400°F; set oven rack to upper third position. Warm oil in large saucepan over medium-low heat. Add onion, chili powder, cumin, salt and pepper; cook 6 minutes, until onions are softened, stirring often. Stir in tomato paste until absorbed.

2. Add beef and cook 5 minutes, until no longer pink. Use a wooden spoon to break up meat as it cooks. Stir in tomatoes and beans. Bring to a simmer; reduce heat and cook, covered, about 10 minutes. Uncover, cook 10 minutes longer, adding a little water if mixture seems dry and stirring occasionally. Season with salt. Pour into a 2-quart casserole or several small oven-safe baking pans.

3. In a large bowl, toss potatoes with salt and pepper. Scatter potatoes over casserole; sprinkle with cheese. Place on a rimmed baking sheet. Bake 35 minutes, until potatoes are cooked through and chili is bubbling. If small pans are used, reduce cooking time.

Serves 4

2 tablespoons olive oil

1 medium onion, chopped

2 tablespoons chili powder

2 teaspoons ground cumin

Salt and pepper, to taste

¼ cup tomato paste

1 pound ground beef

1 15-ounce can diced tomatoes

1 15-ounce can red kidney beans, rinsed and drained

1 pound frozen shredded hash brown potatoes

1 cup shredded cheddar cheese

TIP

You don't need to thaw or precook the potatoes for this dish. If you want the topping to be extra-crispy, dot the potatoes with butter before putting them in the oven.

Roast Chicken with Root Vegetables and Cider Gravy

Serves 4 to 6

1 whole chicken (about 4 pounds)

Salt and pepper, to taste

4 whole garlic cloves, peeled and smashed with the back of a knife

Fresh thyme sprigs

2 tablespoons unsalted butter, at room temperature

1 pound red boiling potatoes, cut into quarters

1 medium onion, coarsely chopped

1 pound carrots, peeled and cut into 1-inch rounds

2 cups apple cider

A basic, foolproof recipe for everyone's favorite Sunday-night dinner.

1. Preheat oven to 400°F. Set a V-rack in a large roasting pan.
2. Rinse chicken; pat dry with paper towel. Season cavity with salt, pepper, garlic and a few sprigs of thyme. Smear chicken skin with butter; set on rack in pan. Surround chicken with vegetables, season with salt and pepper and pour cider over vegetables.
3. Roast 1¾ hours, until vegetables are tender and juices run clear when a chicken leg is pricked with a knife. The thigh meat should register 180°F on an instant-read thermometer.
4. Remove chicken to platter. Using a slotted spoon, transfer vegetables to platter around the chicken. Set roasting pan over high heat and bring pan juices to a boil, scraping up the browned bits on the bottom of the pan. Cook, uncovered, 5 to 10 minutes, until liquid is reduced by half. Pour into gravy boat and serve with chicken.

TIP

This recipe is endlessly adaptable—replace the potatoes with turnips, parsnips or celery root, use chicken broth in place of the cider, add lemons to the filling of the chicken cavity.

Broccoli Casserole with Parmesan Bread Topping

This warm, creamy casserole is a sure-fire way to get the family to enjoy super-healthy broccoli.

1. For topping: In food processor, pulse bread, Parmesan and butter until mixture resembles coarse crumbs.
2. For filling: Preheat oven to 350°F. Melt butter in a medium saucepan over medium heat. Add onion; cook 4 minutes, until softened. Sprinkle in flour, stirring until incorporated. Slowly pour in milk, stirring constantly. Add broccoli; season with salt and pepper. Bring to a gentle simmer; reduce heat to low; cover and cook 5 minutes, until tender-crisp, stirring so milk doesn't scorch. Remove from heat; stir in nutmeg and Jarlsberg.
3. Transfer mixture to a 2-quart casserole; sprinkle with breadcrumb mixture. Cover with foil, bake 15 minutes. Remove foil; bake 15 minutes longer, until breadcrumbs are golden.

My son, Will Jefferson, hates broccoli, but he'll eat this.

Serves 4

TOPPING

2 slices sandwich bread, torn in pieces

2 tablespoons grated Parmesan cheese

1 tablespoon unsalted butter, at room temperature

FILLING

3 tablespoons unsalted butter

½ small onion, finely chopped

⅓ cup all-purpose flour

1¾ cups whole milk

1 bunch broccoli (about 1½ pounds), cut into small florets and stalks thinly sliced

Salt and pepper, to taste

Ground nutmeg, pinch

1 cup shredded Jarlsberg or Swiss cheese

> **TIP**
>
> When buying broccoli, look for bunches with the darkest green color. This recipe uses the entire head; just remember to chop the stalks into smaller pieces than the florets, which cook more quickly.

Stuffed Sweet Peppers

Serves 4

4 small bell peppers, left whole, cored and seeded

½ cup long-grain white rice

1 tablespoon olive oil

1 medium onion, finely chopped

1 14-ounce can diced tomatoes, drained

2 cloves garlic, minced

1 cup shredded Monterey Jack cheese

3 tablespoons chopped fresh parsley

Salt and pepper, to taste

TIP

To easily scrape out the white membrane inside the pepper, use a melon baller.

Green peppers are traditional in this dish, but you may also use a variety of red, yellow and orange peppers, which are sweeter. Paired with golden caramelized onions and mellow tomatoes, this way-back classic deserves a place at any modern dinner table.

1. Bring 4 quarts salted water to a boil in a large stockpot over high heat. Add peppers. Cook 3 minutes, until peppers start to soften. Using slotted spoon or tongs, remove peppers and drain out any water that has collected inside pepper cavities. Place peppers cut-side up in a 9-inch-square baking pan. Return water to a boil; add rice, reduce heat and cook 15 minutes or until tender. Drain.

2. Preheat oven to 350°F. Warm oil in a large heavy skillet over medium-low heat. Add onions; cook 6 minutes, until softened, stirring often. Stir in tomatoes and garlic; cook 2 minutes, stirring. Remove from heat; stir in cooked rice, ¾ cup of the cheese, parsley, salt and pepper.

3. Spoon filling into peppers. Sprinkle remaining ¼ cup cheese evenly over top. Bake 20 minutes, until cheese is melted and filling is heated through.

Spaghetti with Fresh Clam Sauce

Serves 4

1 cup dry white wine, or more
as needed

2 dozen littleneck clams, rinsed

1 pound spaghetti

3 tablespoons olive oil

3 cloves garlic, minced

¾ cup chopped fresh parsley

TIP

When buying clams, look for
shells that are unbroken, free of
cracks and closed. If the shells
are open, the clam is probably
no longer alive.

If you can find fresh clams, treat your family and friends to
this classic pasta dish.

1. Place a large saucepot over medium-high heat; add wine and bring
to a simmer (pour in a little more wine if it looks like there's not
enough liquid to cook the clams). Add clams; cook 5 to 10 minutes,
until shells open. Using tongs, transfer opened clams to a large
bowl. Discard any clams that don't open. Separate clams from
shells, returning any juices to the cooking pot; discard shells.
2. Pour clam cooking broth through a fine strainer set over a large
bowl. Discard solids in strainer.
3. Cook pasta according to package directions. Drain.
4. Warm oil in clam cooking pot over medium-low heat. Cook garlic
about 1 minute, until fragrant. Add clams and strained broth and
warm to simmer. Add pasta and parsley and toss until combined.
Transfer to large serving bowl.

*The secret here is to
make sure the clams
are really fresh. I
buy mine at the
Farmer's Market.*

Anytime Spaghetti with Clams

Fresh clams aren't always available—but a good sauce is still possible. This sauce is spicy—adjust the amount of chili peppers according to your family's tastes.

1. Warm oil in a large heavy skillet over medium heat. Add chili peppers, onion, garlic, salt and pepper; cook 5 minutes, stirring. Add basil, oregano and the clam liquid. Simmer 10 minutes.
2. While sauce simmers, cook pasta according to package directions. Drain.
3. Add clams to sauce; cook until warmed through.
4. In large serving bowl, toss pasta with clam sauce. Garnish with parsley.

Serves 4 to 6

¼ cup olive oil

1–2 red chili peppers, seeded and finely chopped (or crushed red-pepper flakes to taste)

1 medium onion, chopped

3–5 garlic cloves, minced

Salt and pepper, to taste

½ cup chopped fresh basil

2 tablespoons chopped fresh oregano or 1 tablespoon dried oregano

2 cans (4½ to 6-ounce size) chopped clams, liquid drained and reserved

1 pound spaghetti

¾ cup chopped fresh parsley, to garnish

TIP

Canned clams work well in quick-cooking recipes like this one. Their texture is too soft, however, for longer-cooking soups and stews.

Southwestern Taco Salad with Charred Corn

Serves 4 to 6

3 medium flour tortillas, each cut into 16 wedges

1 tablespoon plus 1 teaspoon olive oil

3 ears corn, kernels scraped from the cob

1 pound ground chuck

1 cup canned black beans, drained and rinsed

1 cup prepared salsa

1 teaspoon chili powder

1 teaspoon ground cumin

Salt and pepper, to taste

Juice of 2 limes

¾ cup plain yogurt or sour cream

¼ cup chopped fresh cilantro

3 cups iceberg lettuce, torn or chopped into 2-inch pieces (about ½ pound)

1 small avocado, peeled, seeded, and cut into thin wedges

Use this basic recipe as a jumping-off point; make it your own by using a spicy salsa, adding jalapeños, fresh tomatoes or shredded cheese.

1. Preheat oven to 350°F. Spread tortilla wedges in a single layer on a rimmed baking sheet; drizzle with 1 tablespoon of the oil. Bake about 10 minutes, until crisp, turning once. Remove from oven; let cool.
2. Warm 1 teaspoon oil in a large nonstick skillet over medium heat. Add corn kernels; cook 3 minutes, stirring until slightly charred on both sides. Transfer kernels to a bowl.
3. In same skillet over medium heat, cook beef 6 minutes, until no longer pink, stirring often. Stir in charred corn, beans, salsa, chili powder, cumin, salt and pepper and ½ of the lime juice.
4. Meanwhile, in a small bowl, whisk yogurt or sour cream, remaining lime juice and cilantro until blended.
5. In a large serving bowl, toss lettuce and avocado. Nestle beef mixture in center of salad; drizzle with yogurt dressing. Garnish servings with tortillas.

TIP

To safely scrape kernels from an ear of corn, stand the ear on its end and slice downward with a serrated or sharp chef knife.

Broccoli Lasagna

Serves 6 to 8

1 large head broccoli, cut into small florets and stalks chopped

1 8-ounce container ricotta cheese

1 large egg

Salt and pepper, to taste

4 tablespoons (½ stick) unsalted butter, plus more for coating pan

1 medium onion, chopped

3 cloves garlic, minced

¼ cup all-purpose flour

3¼ cups whole milk

1 cup grated Parmesan cheese, divided

12 no-boil lasagna noodles

2 cups shredded sharp cheddar cheese

TIP

Making a cream sauce is all about patience. Keep stirring as you slowly pour in the milk. In time it will thicken.

This recipe uses the no-boil variety of noodles. If unavailable, cook the regular kind and continue the recipe as written, omitting the soaking.

1. Cook broccoli in boiling water in a medium saucepan until tender-crisp, about 6 minutes. Drain in colander; run cool water over broccoli to stop cooking. Coarsely chop; set aside.

2. In food processor or blender, blend ricotta, egg, salt and pepper until smooth; set aside.

3. Melt butter in same saucepan over medium-low heat. Add onion and garlic; cook 4 minutes, until softened, stirring. Sprinkle in flour and cook until incorporated, stirring constantly, about 1 minute. Do not brown. Slowly stir in milk; bring to a simmer. Reduce heat and simmer 10 minutes, until thickened to the consistency of heavy cream, stirring often. Remove from heat; stir in salt, pepper and ½ cup of the Parmesan.

4. Preheat oven to 425°F; set oven rack to middle position. Place noodles in 13-by-9-inch baking pan; cover with hot tap water. Let soak 5 minutes, gently shaking pan to prevent sticking. Remove noodles from water; lay on kitchen towel or paper towels to blot dry. Empty water from pan; wipe dry and rub with butter.

5. Spread ½ cup white sauce in bottom of pan; lay 3 noodles on top of sauce. Stir broccoli into remaining white sauce; you should have about 4 cups. Spread 1 cup of this broccoli mixture evenly over noodles. Sprinkle with remaining ½ cup Parmesan, and top with 3 more noodles. Spread 1 cup broccoli mixture over noodles, sprinkle with 1 cup cheddar, and top with 3 more noodles. Spread 1 cup broccoli mixture over noodles, top with ricotta mixture. Finish with 3 noodles, remaining broccoli mixture and remaining cheddar.

6. Cover pan with foil. Bake 20 minutes, until bubbling. Remove from oven; take off foil. Heat broiler. Broil lasagna about 5 minutes, until cheese browns. Cool 10 minutes before serving.

Garlic Bread

This classic garlic bread is the ideal accompaniment to any pasta dish. Feel free to up the cheese, if desired.

1. Preheat oven to 450°F. In a small dry skillet over medium-low heat, toast whole garlic cloves 6 minutes, until cloves turn golden, shaking pan often. Transfer to cutting board; crush cloves with the side of a knife. Peel and mince garlic.
2. In a small bowl, use a fork to mash garlic, butter, cheese and salt until combined.
3. Using a serrated knife, slice bread in half lengthwise. Spread cut sides with garlic mixture. Place on baking sheet, buttered-side up. Bake 10 minutes, until golden brown.

Serves 8–10

8 cloves garlic, unpeeled

5 tablespoons unsalted butter, at room temperature

¼ cup grated Parmesan cheese

Salt, to taste

1 loaf Italian bread, 12 to 16 ounces

TIP

Serve the crispy, crunchy bread warm from the oven.

Don't spare the garlic. It's good for you, or so Olivia tells me.

Teri's Macaroni and Cheese

This rich, super-cheesy dish is a meal the whole family will love.

Serves 6 to 8

1. Preheat oven to 350°F. Butter a 3-quart casserole pan or several small oven-safe baking cups.
2. Melt butter in a medium saucepan over medium-low heat. Sprinkle in flour; stir until absorbed, about 1 minute. Slowly pour in milk, stirring constantly, until incorporated. Reduce heat to low, add Velveeta chunks, stirring until melted. Stir in cottage cheese, sour cream, salt and pepper.
3. Meanwhile, cook macaroni according to package directions. Drain; place in prepared pan. Fold in cheese sauce. Cover and bake 25 minutes. Uncover, sprinkle with shredded cheddar and bake 10 minutes, until cheese melts.

4 tablespoons (½ stick) butter, plus extra for the pan

⅓ cup all-purpose flour

2 cups whole milk

½ pound Velveeta cheese, cut into chunks

½ cup cottage cheese

½ cup sour cream

Salt and pepper, to taste

1 pound elbow macaroni

Shredded cheddar cheese, for topping

This is comfort food at its best. Must work well as a fertility drug too, since Teri's pregnant with triplets.

TIP

For heartier appetites, stir in some chopped ham or cooked beef with taco seasonings before baking.

Shrimp Enchilada Bake with Ricotta and Monterey Jack

Serves 4 to 6

1 16-ounce container whole milk ricotta cheese

2 cups shredded Monterey Jack cheese

1 pound medium shelled and deveined shrimp, cooked and halved

5 scallions, thinly sliced

½ cup chopped fresh cilantro

Salt and pepper, to taste

8 medium flour tortillas

Bottled tomatillo sauce or other green chili sauce

Bottled red chili sauce

TIP

Save time by using frozen shrimp, which is already shelled and deveined.

This simple meal is in the oven in 10 minutes.

1. Preheat oven to 350°F. Lightly coat a 2-quart casserole with nonstick spray.
2. In a large bowl, combine ricotta, Monterey Jack, shrimp, scallions, cilantro, salt and pepper.
3. Lay tortillas out on countertop. Evenly fill tortillas with shrimp mixture. Carefully roll up. Place tortillas, seam-side down, in prepared pan. Lightly drizzle red and green sauces over tortillas in an alternate pattern. Cover pan with foil; bake 30 minutes, until hot.

Rosie tells me this is a great Friday night dish and Zach loves it.

Fried Chicken

The key to crisp fried chicken is cooking at a high temperature. Stick a candy or deep-frying thermometer in the chicken as you fry to make sure the oil temperature remains between 250° and 300°F.

1. Rinse chicken. In a large bowl or resealable plastic bag, combine buttermilk and Tabasco. Add chicken pieces, turn to coat. Refrigerate; covered, for at least 8 hours and up to 16, turning the pieces occasionally. Remove chicken from buttermilk; shake off excess. Arrange in a single layer on large wire rack set over rimmed baking sheet. Refrigerate, uncovered, for 2 hours. (After 2 hours, chicken can be covered with plastic wrap and refrigerated up to 6 hours longer.)

2. Measure flour into large shallow dish; whisk in some salt and pepper. In a medium bowl, beat eggs, baking powder and baking soda. Working in batches of 3, drop chicken pieces in flour and shake dish to coat. Shake excess flour from each piece. Using tongs, dip chicken pieces into egg mixture, turning to coat well and allowing excess to drip off. Return chicken pieces to flour; coat again, shake off excess, and set on wire rack.

3. Preheat oven to 200°F. Set oven rack to middle position. Set another wire rack over a rimmed baking sheet, and place in oven. Line a large plate with paper towels. Pour oil about ½ inch up the side of a large, heavy skillet. Place skillet over high heat; let pan warm until oil shimmers.

4. Place half of chicken, skin-side down, in hot oil. Reduce heat to medium and fry 8 minutes, until deep golden brown. Turn chicken pieces; cook an additional 8 minutes, turning to fry evenly on all sides. Using tongs, transfer chicken to paper-towel-lined plate. After draining, transfer chicken to wire rack in oven. Fry remaining chicken, transferring pieces to paper-towel-lined plate to drain, then to wire rack in oven to keep warm.

Serves 4 to 6

1 whole chicken (about 3½ pounds), cut into 10 pieces

1 quart buttermilk

2 tablespoons Tabasco or other hot sauce

2 cups all-purpose flour

Salt and pepper, to taste

2 large eggs

1 teaspoon baking powder

½ teaspoon baking soda

Vegetable oil or shortening

TIP

For ease of frying, cut the breasts in half, for a total of 10 pieces.

Caesar Salad with Lemon Shrimp and Homemade Garlic Croutons

Serves 4

CROUTONS

2 tablespoons olive oil

1 clove garlic, minced

Salt, to taste

6 slices sandwich bread, cut into ½-inch cubes

SHRIMP

2 tablespoons olive oil

1 pound large shrimp, peeled and deveined (thawed if frozen)

2 teaspoons lemon zest

2 tablespoons fresh lemon juice

Salt and pepper, to taste

2 small heads Romaine lettuce, trimmed and torn into 2-inch pieces

Prepared Caesar salad dressing, to taste

Using a prepared salad dressing and shelled, deveined shrimp shortens the prep time for this favorite salad.

1. For croutons: Preheat oven to 350°F. In a medium bowl, combine oil, minced garlic and salt; let stand 5 minutes. Add bread cubes; toss to coat. Spread in an even layer on a rimmed baking sheet. Bake 15 minutes, until golden, stirring occasionally. Cool on baking sheet.

2. For shrimp: Warm oil in a large skillet with a lid over medium heat. Add shrimp and lemon zest. Cover and cook 5 minutes, stirring occasionally, until shrimp are opaque. Remove from heat; stir in lemon juice, salt and pepper.

3. In a large serving bowl, toss lettuce and dressing to coat. Heap on the shrimp and croutons; serve immediately.

TIP

Because Caesar salad dressing is thick, this recipe calls for sturdy Romaine lettuce.

I'm not one to brag, but my croutons are fabulous. It's all about the cast-iron skillet.

Creamy Risotto with Spring Vegetables

Serves 8

3 tablespoons olive oil, divided

8 ounces sugar snap peas, trimmed and halved

1 small zucchini, trimmed, cut into 1-inch pieces

Salt and pepper, to taste

6 cups reduced-sodium chicken broth, or as needed

1 small onion, chopped

1 carrot, peeled and diced small

1½ cups Arborio rice or medium-grain white rice

¾ cup dry white wine

1 cup grated Parmesan cheese, plus additional for garnish

1 cup frozen peas or shelled edamame, thawed

4 tablespoons (½ stick) butter, cut into chunks

½ cup chopped fresh dill

TIP

This is a big-batch recipe. Cook it in a big pot, since the rice expands as it cooks.

There's no trick to making risotto—all you need is a little time and a strong stirring arm.

1. Warm 1 tablespoon oil in a large heavy skillet over medium-high heat. Add snap peas, zucchini, salt and pepper. Cook 3 minutes, stirring. Set aside in a small bowl.

2. Bring broth and 2 cups water to simmer in a medium saucepan over low heat. Cover to keep warm.

3. In the same skillet used for the vegetables, warm remaining 2 tablespoons oil over medium-high heat. Add onion and carrot. Cook 5 minutes, until softened, stirring often. Add rice; cook 2 minutes, until rice is coated and translucent around the edges. Add wine and simmer about 3 minutes, until absorbed, stirring occasionally.

4. Stir 1 cup warm broth into rice. Simmer until broth is almost absorbed, about 3 minutes, stirring constantly. Keep adding broth to rice, 1 cup at a time, allowing each addition to be absorbed before adding next and stirring frequently, about 20 minutes, until only about 1½ cups of broth remain.

5. Add sautéed vegetables and 1 cup broth. Simmer 5 minutes, until broth is just absorbed, stirring often. Add cheese, peas, butter and ½ cup broth (if you have run out of broth, add water). Simmer about 3 minutes, until rice and vegetables are just tender. Keep stirring and add more broth if needed. Risotto should be creamy. Stir in dill; season with salt and pepper. Garnish with cheese.

Cauliflower, Potato and Cheese Soup

R ich and cheesy, this soup makes a hearty and soothing supper.

Serves 6

1. Melt butter in a large Dutch oven over medium heat until foaming. Add leeks and cook 15 minutes, stirring occasionally, until tender. Sprinkle flour over leeks and cook, until flour is incorporated, stirring constantly.
2. Increase heat to high; gradually add broth, stirring constantly. Add potatoes, cauliflower and bay leaf; cover and bring to boil. Reduce heat to medium-low and simmer 10 minutes, covered, until vegetables are almost tender.
3. Remove from heat. Stir in shredded cheese and season to taste with salt and pepper.

Emily Flemming has some wonderful recipes from all those church dinners, and this is one of them.

4 tablespoons (½ stick) unsalted butter

4 leeks, white and light green parts only, thinly sliced and well rinsed

1 tablespoon all-purpose flour

5 cups (or more) reduced-sodium vegetable or chicken broth

3 large russet potatoes (about 1½ pounds), peeled, diced

1 small head cauliflower (about 1 pound), trimmed, cut into florets

1 bay leaf

1 cup shredded Gruyère or Swiss cheese

Salt and pepper, to taste

TIP

Clean gritty leeks by slicing them and then rinsing in a strainer under cold running water, separating the rings with your fingers.

Penne with Caramelized Butternut Squash and Parmesan

Mellow butternut squash and sharp Parmesan make for a delicious change-of-pace winter pasta dish.

Serves 4 to 6

1. Cook pasta according to package directions. Drain, reserving 1 cup pasta cooking water.
2. Meanwhile, melt 3 tablespoons of the butter in a large heavy saucepan over medium-high heat. Arrange squash chunks in a single layer; cook 6 minutes, without stirring. Turn cubes; cook 4 minutes. Add broth, brown sugar, salt and pepper. Cover pan and cook 4 minutes. Uncover; cook 3 minutes, until most of liquid has evaporated and squash is tender. Transfer squash and any liquid to large shallow serving bowl.
3. Warm remaining 2 tablespoons butter in same skillet over medium-low heat. Add leeks; cook 5 minutes, stirring often. Return squash to pot; stir in thyme and vinegar. Stir in reserved pasta cooking water to desired consistency.
4. In a large serving bowl, toss pasta with squash. Garnish with cheese.

1 pound penne or other tube pasta

5 tablespoons unsalted butter, divided

1 large butternut squash (about 3 pounds), peeled, seeded and cut into ¾-inch chunks

1 cup reduced-sodium chicken broth

1 tablespoon brown sugar

Salt and pepper, to taste

2 leeks, thinly sliced and well rinsed (or 1 small onion, diced)

2 teaspoons chopped fresh thyme or 1 teaspoon dried whole thyme

1 teaspoon sherry or red-wine vinegar

½ cup shaved or grated Parmesan cheese, for garnish

TIP

The skin of butternut squash is very hard; you'll need a heavy knife to slice it. You can microwave the squash for 2 minutes to make it easier to cut. Poke a few holes in the skin before microwaving.

Italian Braised Chicken with Peppers, Onions and Sweet Sausage

Serves 4 to 6

2 pounds bone-in, skin-on chicken breast halves

Salt and pepper, to taste

3 teaspoons olive oil, divided

8 ounces sweet Italian sausage, or a combination of sweet and spicy sausage

2 red bell peppers, cored and thinly sliced

1 large onion, thinly sliced

4 cloves garlic, minced

1 cup reduced-sodium chicken broth

¼ cup white- or red-wine vinegar

1 tablespoon granulated sugar

1 teaspoon cornstarch or flour

2 teaspoons chopped fresh thyme or 1 teaspoon dried thyme

TIP

Use a large, deep skillet or a Dutch oven to hold all the chicken and vegetables and prevent splattering.

Serve this simple but satisfying dish over noodles or alongside boiled or mashed potatoes.

1. Preheat oven to 350°F; set oven rack at middle position. Using a sharp, heavy knife, cut breasts in half crosswise. Season chicken with salt and pepper.

2. Warm 1 teaspoon of the oil in a large heavy ovenproof skillet over medium heat. Add sausage; cook 4 minutes, breaking up the meat with the back of a spoon while it cooks (sausage will not be cooked through). Transfer to a paper-towel-lined plate to drain.

3. Warm remaining 2 teaspoons oil in same skillet over medium-high heat. Add chicken, skin-side down. Cook 4 minutes, without moving. Flip chicken; cook 3 minutes, until browned. Transfer chicken to large plate.

4. Set same skillet over medium heat. Add bell peppers, onion, salt and pepper; cook 7 minutes, stirring often. Add garlic and cook 30 seconds, stirring. Add broth, vinegar and sugar; bring mixture to boil, scraping up browned bits from pan bottom.

5. Return sausage and chicken (with any accumulated juices) to skillet, arranging chicken pieces in single layer, skin-side up, on top of peppers and onion. Transfer skillet to oven and cook 20 to 22 minutes, until instant-read thermometer inserted into thickest part of chicken registers 160°F.

6. Remove skillet from oven. Transfer chicken and larger pieces of sausage and vegetables to serving platter. Place skillet over medium-high heat; sprinkle with cornstarch and thyme. Simmer 3 minutes, until sauce is slightly thickened. Season with salt and pepper. Spoon sauce around chicken and vegetables on platter.

Braised Halibut in Roman-Style Sauce

Serve this Italian-inspired dish with rice or potatoes.

Serves 4

1. Warm oil in a large heavy skillet over medium-high heat. Season fish with salt and pepper; set in pan, skin-side down. Cook 4 minutes, until browned on the bottom. Turn fillets; cook 3 minutes, until browned. Fish will not be cooked through. Remove to large serving platter.

2. Place same skillet over medium heat. Add peppers and prosciutto; cook 5 minutes, until browned, stirring. Add garlic; cook 30 seconds, stirring. Add tomatoes, wine and oregano. Using a wooden spoon, scrape browned bits from bottom of pan.

3. Return halibut to pan, setting fish on top of vegetables. Bring to a simmer; reduce heat and cook, covered, 6 minutes, until fish is cooked through. Check midway through cooking time; add water to pan if sauce is drying out too much. Ladle sauce onto serving plates; top with fillets. Garnish servings with capers and parsley.

2 tablespoons olive oil

4 halibut fillets, about 5 ounces each

Salt and pepper, to taste

2 bell peppers, preferably red and yellow, cored and sliced

2 ounces prosciutto, chopped

3 cloves garlic, chopped

1 15-ounce can diced tomatoes

½ cup dry white wine

2 teaspoons chopped fresh oregano

2 tablespoons drained capers

½ cup chopped fresh parsley, for garnish

Like I said, Italians know their pasta—and their fish. Chianti goes well with this meal.

TIP

Because halibut is so lean, it's important that you don't overcook the tender fillets or they will dry out.

Roasted Garlic White Pizza

Serves 6

1 head garlic

2 teaspoons olive oil, divided, plus extra for pan

Salt and pepper, to taste

2 tablespoons unsalted butter

2 tablespoons all-purpose flour

¾ cup whole milk

1 bunch or bag (10 to 12 ounces) fresh spinach

Cornmeal, for pan

1 ball prepared pizza dough (about 1 pound)

8 ounces fresh mozzarella, shredded

4 ounces shredded Fontina or Jarlsberg cheese

TIP

Using the pizza dough from your local pizzeria makes for a professional-looking and super-easy pie. Many supermarkets also offer prepared pizza dough in 1-pound balls in the refrigerated section.

Garlic turns super-sweet when roasted; here, roasted garlic is blended into a creamy white sauce for pizza.

1. Preheat oven to 350°F. Line an 8-inch-square baking pan with foil. Slice off the top quarter of the garlic head (the narrower end, not the fatter base). Drizzle about 1 teaspoon oil over the cut side of the head; sprinkle with salt and pepper. Place in prepared pan, cut-side down. Bake 1 hour, until cloves are soft when squeezed. Remove from oven; let sit until cool enough to handle. Squeeze head, cut-side down, to release the garlic purée into a small bowl.

2. Melt butter in a small saucepan over medium-low heat. Sprinkle in flour; stir until incorporated. Slowly pour in milk, stirring constantly until mixture thickens. Remove from heat; whisk in garlic purée, pressing any lumps against the side of the pan to incorporate them into the sauce. Season with salt and pepper.

3. Warm remaining 1 teaspoon oil in a medium saucepan over medium heat. Add spinach; cook 5 minutes, until wilted, stirring often. Turn out onto cutting board; coarsely chop.

4. Preheat oven to 425°F. Lightly coat a large baking sheet with oil; sprinkle with cornmeal. On lightly floured countertop, roll out pizza dough to a 15-inch round or 12-by-14-inch rectangle. Transfer to prepared pan. Let dough rest 15 minutes.

5. Spread white sauce evenly over pizza crust. Drop spinach over sauce; sprinkle with mozzarella and Fontina or Jarlsberg.

6. Bake 15 minutes, until crust is golden and cheese melts.

Rosemary-Garlic Crusted Pork Tenderloin on Sautéed Spinach

Serves 4 to 6

3 tablespoons olive oil

6 cloves garlic

3 tablespoons chopped fresh rosemary

Salt and pepper, to taste

2 pork tenderloins (about 1½ pounds total)

1 large bunch or bag (10 to 16 ounces) fresh spinach, washed but not dried

¾ cup reduced-sodium chicken broth

TIP

Using a sharp knife, carefully slice off the shiny membrane (called the silverskin) attached to each tenderloin. Leaving it on can cause the meat to toughen.

Pork tenderloin is usually sold in packages of two. As long as you are in the kitchen, you may as well cook them both. Round out the meal by serving the pork and spinach on a bed of mashed potatoes.

1. Preheat oven to 400°F. In food processor, pulse oil, garlic, rosemary, salt and pepper until a paste forms. Using your hands, rub tenderloins with most of the garlic paste; reserving about 1 tablespoon.

2. Set a large ovenproof skillet over high heat. Sear tenderloins on all sides, about 8 minutes, until browned. Transfer skillet to oven; roast 25 minutes, until thermometer inserted into thickest part registers 150°F.

3. Meanwhile, place remaining garlic paste in a large heavy saucepan over medium-high heat. Add spinach; cook 4 minutes, until wilted, stirring often. Stir in chicken broth; continue to cook 2 minutes, stirring often.

4. Transfer pork to cutting board and slice. Pour any pan juices from pork skillet into spinach. Divide spinach among 4 plates. Top with pork slices.

Corrie McAfee told me this is Roy's favorite Sunday dinner—and he's not an easy man to please.

Chicken and Wild Rice Soup with Leeks

This big-batch soup feeds a crowd. Serve it with some crusty bread and a leafy green salad.

1. In a large soup pot, combine chicken, carrots, onions, bay leaves, peppercorns and salt. Add water to cover by at least 2 inches. Bring to a boil; reduce heat and simmer, partly covered, for about 1 hour. If needed, skim any fat that collects on the surface.
2. Using tongs, remove chicken and carrots from pot; place on cutting board. Pour remaining contents of pot through a strainer set over a big bowl. Discard solids in strainer; pour cooking broth back into pot. Bring to a boil over high heat. Add rice; reduce heat to medium and simmer, uncovered, 50 minutes or until rice is tender.
3. Meanwhile, remove and discard skin and bones from chicken. Shred meat into bite-size pieces. Cut cooked carrots into bite-size chunks.
4. Melt 1 tablespoon butter in medium saucepan over medium-high heat. Add leeks and cook 6 minutes, until softened, stirring often.
5. Return chicken and carrots to pot. Add leeks. Simmer until warmed through and flavors combined, about 10 minutes. Season with salt, pepper and chopped dill.

Serves 10

1 whole chicken (3 to 4 pounds)

1 pound carrots, peeled and cut in half

2 large onions, halved

2 bay leaves

1 tablespoon whole peppercorns

Salt and pepper, to taste

1½ cups wild rice

1 tablespoon unsalted butter

2 leeks, thinly sliced

Chopped fresh dill, for garnish

TIP

Get a head start by cooking the chicken and rice a day in advance. The next day, simmer them briefly with the leeks and you'll have hot soup in minutes!

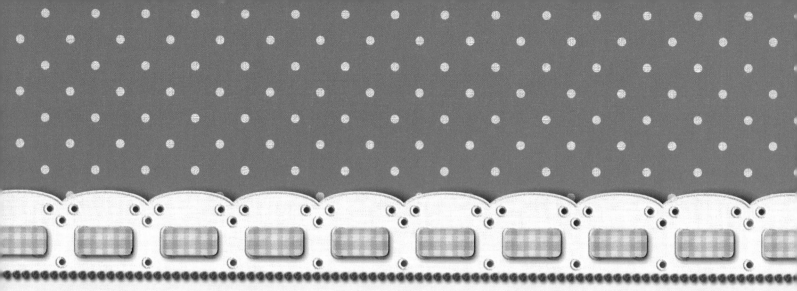

Dessert

at **50 HARBOR STREET** *with*

Roy and Corrie McAfee

This is my very favorite section! Desserts.

I'd venture to say that one of the reasons Ben and I hit it off so quickly is that he, too, has a notorious sweet tooth. I do love my desserts, so you won't be surprised to hear that I have an extensive collection of recipes. Several of my favorites came from Corrie McAfee. She tells me Roy isn't nearly as fond of sweets as she is, but she ignores that and doesn't let it stop her from experimenting with new desserts.

Corrie and Peggy Beldon have become good friends and they frequently exchange recipes. Peggy insists on ending her fabulous dinners with just the right dessert; she says the meal wouldn't be complete otherwise. Now, that's my kind of woman! And Corrie McAfee feels exactly the same way.

The McAfees moved to Cedar Cove a few years ago. Roy was a Seattle police detective forced into early retirement because of a back injury he sustained while on duty. I only know about this because Corrie mentioned it, but every now and then I see him pressing his fists into his lower back, a sure sign that he's in pain.

A year or so after they moved here, Roy hung out his shingle as a Private Investigator. That raised a lot of questions, because Cedar Cove had never had a P.I. before. People wondered what he'd find to investigate in a peaceful town like ours but, as it turns out, Roy's found more than enough work.

Since he was in law enforcement for so long, it's only natural, I suppose, that he'd strike up a friendship with Sheriff Troy Davis. Fortunately the sheriff sees him as an ally, not a competitor, and I know Roy respects the professional boundaries between them. I often see them chatting over a cup of coffee at the Pot Belly Deli.

After Roy and Corrie moved to town, their children followed. Linnette was one of the first employees at the Cedar Cove Medical Center, although she lives in North Dakota now, working at a medical clinic in a small town called Buffalo Valley. Mack's a local firefighter. Roy and Corrie have an older daughter, too—Gloria, who recently joined our Sheriff's Department. Gloria came into their lives just a few years ago, but that's a whole other story and I'll let Corrie tell you about it.

Most days, you can catch up with Corrie at Roy's office, where she serves as his administrative assistant (in my day we referred to that as a secretary). If you drop in—I hope it's not because you need Roy's services!—be sure to ask about her favorite dessert recipes.

Coconut Layer Cake is one I gave her. I've been serving it for years and I can promise you it never fails to please a crowd. Ben loves it, and the first time Corrie tasted it she became a convert, too.

And speaking of coconut, anyone who knows Olivia and Grace will remember how much they love Coconut Cream Pie. Every Wednesday night after their aerobics class they go to the Pancake Palace for coffee and a slice of pie. Confidentially, my recipe's better. I don't think I'll get either of them to admit it, but Peggy's on my side in this.

Let me mention just a couple more. First, Corrie's Oatmeal Date Bars. She told me they were Mack's favorite from when he was five years old. Apparently Roy won't touch them and never has. Well, that's his loss and our gain (in more ways than one!). According to Olivia and Jack, Corrie's Russian Tea Cakes are as good as those from the bakery—and they should know.

Take a few minutes to read through these recipes, and for heaven's sake don't worry about calories! There's always tomorrow. Life should be enjoyed, and that means indulging yourself once in a while. That's what Ben says and I agree with him. So does Corrie McAfee…even if Roy doesn't.

Lattice-Top Cherry Pie

Makes 1 9" pie

²⁄₃ cup granulated sugar, plus extra for crust

3 tablespoons cornstarch or flour

1 tablespoon orange juice

1 teaspoon ground cinnamon

Pinch salt

24 ounces frozen pitted sweet dark cherries, thawed and drained or 5 cups pitted fresh cherries (about 2½ pounds)

2 refrigerated or frozen pie crusts, thawed

1 egg white, lightly beaten

TIP

Use any sharp knife to cut the lattice strips; to make scalloped-edged strips, use a fluted pastry wheel.

Using frozen or fresh cherries for your pie will be a revelation if you've only ever used canned cherry pie filling before.

1. In a large bowl, combine ²⁄₃ cup sugar, cornstarch, orange juice, cinnamon and salt. Add cherries; toss to coat. Let stand 30 minutes.
2. Preheat oven to 400°F. Press one pie crust into a glass 9-inch pie dish. On a lightly floured countertop, roll out second pie crust to a rough rectangle shape. Using a fluted pastry wheel or sharp knife, cut rectangle lengthwise into ten ¾-inch-wide strips.
3. Spoon cherry filling into crust. Place 5 dough strips across pie in 1 direction and 4 in opposite direction, forming a lattice. Press strip ends and edge of crust together to seal. Crimp edges decoratively. Brush lattice and edges with beaten egg. Sprinkle additional sugar over lattice.
4. Bake pie 20 minutes. Cover crust edges with foil to prevent overbrowning. Continue to bake 40 minutes longer, until filling bubbles and crust is golden. Transfer to wire rack to cool.

George Washington—chopper of cherry trees—was on to something good.

New York Cheesecake

Makes 1 9" cake

CRUST

8 whole graham crackers
(about 4 ounces)

2 tablespoons granulated sugar

5 tablespoons unsalted butter,
melted, plus extra for pan

FILLING

2½ pounds cream cheese, at
room temperature, cut into
chunks

1½ cups granulated sugar

Pinch salt

½ cup sour cream

2 teaspoons fresh lemon juice

2 teaspoons vanilla extract

6 large eggs

TIP

Wrap the bottom of the springform pan in heavy-duty foil to
assure that water doesn't soak
through the seal of the pan.

Creamy and luscious, this classic dessert is deceptively easy to make. Prebaking the crumb crust prevents it from becoming soggy. Remember to let it cool completely before adding the filling.

1. Preheat oven to 350°F; set oven rack to lower third position. Lightly coat bottom and sides of a 9-inch springform pan with butter. Wrap the bottom of the pan in heavy-duty foil; the foil should come about halfway up the sides of the pan.

2. For crust: In food processor, pulse graham crackers until fine crumbs form. Add sugar and melted butter; pulse until combined. Press crumbs evenly into bottom of prepared pan. Bake 12 minutes, until edges start to brown. Transfer to wire rack to cool. Keep oven at 350°F.

3. For filling: In a large bowl with electric mixer on high speed, beat cream cheese until blended, scraping sides of bowl. Add sugar and salt; beat until combined. Add sour cream, lemon juice and vanilla; beat until combined. Add eggs one at a time, beating and scraping the bowl between additions.

4. Pour filling into prepared springform pan. Set pan inside a large, shallow roasting pan. Carefully add boiling water to the roasting pan to reach halfway up sides of springform pan.

5. Bake 45 minutes; reduce oven temperature to 325°F. Continue baking 25 minutes longer, until cake is set but still slightly wobbly in the center. Turn off oven; leave door slightly ajar and let cheesecake sit in oven 1 hour. Transfer to wire rack to cool completely. Run a knife around edges to release from pan. Refrigerate at least 6 hours or overnight.

6. Remove pan sides; slide cake (still on its springform base) onto serving plate.

Quick Lemonade Cake

Adding a box of lemon pudding to a lemon-cake mix ensures a super-moist and super-lemony cake.

1. For batter: Preheat oven to 350°F. Lightly grease and flour a large Bundt pan. Make cake according to package directions, adding pudding mix and lemon juice. Pour into prepared pan. Bake as directed on package. Let cool 15 minutes. Carefully run a knife around edges to release from pan. Invert cake onto serving plate.
2. For glaze: In a small bowl, whisk glaze ingredients until smooth. Drizzle over warm cake.

Serves 16

CAKE

1 18-ounce box lemon-flavored cake mix

1 4-ounce box lemon-flavored instant pudding mix

¼ cup fresh lemon juice

GLAZE

1 cup confectioners' sugar

3 tablespoons whole milk

1 tablespoon fresh lemon juice

My aunt Betty, who lived to be over a hundred, gave me this recipe. I wonder if it contributed to her longevity.

TIP

Room-temperature lemons will yield more juice than cold ones. One lemon provides about 3 tablespoons juice.

Celebrations Coconut Layer Cake

Every meal becomes a party when it ends with this beautiful cake. There's no need to worry about making the frosting look perfect since the entire cake is covered with a cloud of coconut flakes.

1. Preheat oven to 350°F. Line two 9-inch cake pans with parchment paper. Lightly butter and flour pans.
2. For batter: In a large bowl with electric mixer on high speed, beat butter and sugar until light and fluffy. Add eggs, one at a time, beating well after each addition. Beat in vanilla and coconut extracts.
3. In a medium bowl, combine flour, baking powder, baking soda and salt. Slowly add this mixture to butter mixture, alternating with the coconut milk. Mix only until blended. Stir in 1½ cups coconut flakes. Pour into prepared pans.
4. Bake 30 minutes, until a toothpick inserted in center comes out clean. Transfer to wire racks to cool. Run a knife around sides of pan, loosening cake from pan. Invert cakes onto wire racks to cool.
5. For frosting: In large bowl with electric mixer on high speed, beat cream cheese, butter and a pinch of salt until combined. Beat in vanilla and coconut extracts. Reduce speed to low; slowly add confectioners' sugar. Beat 5 minutes, until light and fluffy.
6. Frost cake as desired. Cover entire cake with remaining coconut flakes, pressing lightly into cake to make the coconut stick.

TIP

For easy blending, both the cream cheese and the butter should be at room temperature.

Makes 1 9" cake

CAKE

1½ cups (3 sticks) unsalted butter, at room temperature

2 cups granulated sugar

5 large eggs

1½ teaspoons vanilla extract

1½ teaspoons coconut extract

3 cups all-purpose flour

2 teaspoons baking powder

½ teaspoon baking soda

½ teaspoon salt

1 cup unsweetened coconut milk

2½ cups sweetened coconut flakes, divided

FROSTING

8 ounces cream cheese, at room temperature

½ cup (1 stick) unsalted butter, at room temperature

Pinch salt

1 teaspoon vanilla extract

1 teaspoon coconut extract

4 cups confectioners' sugar (about 1 pound)

Sweetened coconut flakes, for garnish

Chocolate Zucchini Cake

Makes 2 9" x 5" loaves

3 large eggs

1 cup vegetable oil

2 cups granulated sugar

2 teaspoons vanilla extract

3 cups grated zucchini
(about 2 medium zucchini)

2⅓ cups all-purpose flour

⅓ cup unsweetened cocoa

2 teaspoons baking soda

1 teaspoon ground cinnamon
(optional)

1 teaspoon salt

¼ teaspoon baking powder

½ cup chopped walnuts
or pecans

½ cup semisweet
chocolate chips

TIP

Since the recipe makes two
loaves, tightly wrap (in plastic
and foil) and freeze one loaf. It
will keep for at least a month.

Dense and moist, this sweet bread makes an excellent afternoon snack or casual dessert.

1. Preheat oven to 350°F. Lightly coat two 9-by-5-inch loaf pans with cooking spray.
2. In a medium bowl, whisk eggs, oil, sugar, vanilla and zucchini until blended. In a large bowl, combine flour, cocoa, baking soda, cinnamon if using, salt and baking powder. Fold the zucchini mix into dry ingredients just until combined. Stir in nuts and chocolate chips. Divide the batter between the prepared loaf pans.
3. Bake 45 to 50 minutes or until toothpick inserted in center comes out clean. Allow to cool 10 minutes in the pans, then turn out onto wire racks to cool completely.

Zucchini grows like crazy here and there's no better way to serve it than in a cake— or so Jack says.

Coconut Cream Pie

Canned coconut milk is a thick blend of coconut meat and water, not to be mistaken for coconut juice, which is the liquid found inside a coconut.

1. For crust: Preheat oven to 325°F; set oven rack to lower-middle position. In food processor, pulse cookies, coconut flakes and butter until fine crumbs form. Press crumbs into bottom and sides of a 9-inch-glass pie dish. Bake 15 minutes, until medium brown, rotating pie shell halfway through baking time. Transfer to wire rack to cool.

2. For filling: In a medium saucepan over medium heat, bring coconut milk, whole milk, coconut flakes, sugar and salt to simmer, stirring often so that sugar dissolves.

3. In a medium bowl, whisk yolks and cornstarch until thoroughly combined. Slowly pour 1 cup hot-milk mixture into yolk mixture; whisk well to combine. Whisking constantly, gradually add remaining milk mixture in 4 additions. Pour mixture back into saucepan over medium heat. Cook 2 minutes, whisking constantly, until mixture thickens and reaches a full boil.

4. Remove pan from heat; whisk in butter, vanilla and coconut extract. Pour hot filling into cooled pie shell. Press plastic wrap directly against surface of filling. Refrigerate until firm, about 3 hours.

5. For topping: Just before serving, beat cream, sugar and coconut extract in a large bowl with electric mixer on high speed until soft peaks form, about 2 minutes. Spread over chilled pie; sprinkle with coconut flakes. Serve cold.

→ TIP

Be sure not to buy cream of coconut instead. It is a sweetened coconut milk and is used mostly for drinks.

Makes one 9" pie

CRUST

6 ounces shortbread cookies

¼ cup sweetened coconut flakes

½ cup (1 stick) unsalted butter, melted

FILLING

1 cup unsweetened coconut milk

1 cup whole milk

½ cup sweetened coconut flakes

⅔ cup granulated sugar

Pinch salt

5 large egg yolks

¼ cup cornstarch

2 tablespoons unsalted butter

1 teaspoon vanilla extract

¼ teaspoon coconut extract

TOPPING

1¼ cups heavy cream

2 tablespoons granulated sugar

⅛ teaspoon coconut extract

⅔ cup sweetened coconut flakes

Apple Pie with Cinnamon Streusel Topping

Makes 1 9" pie

1 refrigerated or frozen pie shell, thawed

TOPPING

1 cup all-purpose flour

⅓ cup granulated sugar

⅓ cup brown sugar

1½ teaspoons ground cinnamon

Pinch salt

½ cup (1 stick) cold unsalted butter, diced

FILLING

1¼ pounds Granny Smith apples (3 to 4 medium apples)

1¼ pounds Macintosh apples (3 to 4 medium apples)

½ cup granulated sugar

2 tablespoons all-purpose flour

¼ teaspoon salt

1 teaspoon ground cinnamon

¼ teaspoon ground nutmeg

The fresher the apples, the better the pie. Because it's impossible to know how long supermarket apples have been stored, use local apples whenever you can.

1. Preheat oven to 400°F; set oven rack to center position. Prick prepared pie shell all over with a fork and line with parchment paper; weigh down with pie weights or uncooked rice. Bake 10 minutes. Remove weights and paper and bake 5 minutes, until golden. Transfer to wire rack to cool. Lower oven temperature to 375°F.

2. For topping: In a food processor, blend flour, white and brown sugars, cinnamon and salt. Add diced butter; pulse until mixture resembles wet sand.

3. For filling: Peel, core and cut apples into thin slices. In a large bowl, toss apples with ½ cup granulated sugar, 2 tablespoons flour, salt, cinnamon and nutmeg. Pour into cooled pie shell, mounding apples in center. Sprinkle topping evenly over apples, mounding if needed.

4. Place pie on a baking sheet and bake 40 minutes. Reduce oven temperature to 350°F. Cover topping with foil to prevent overbrowning. Bake 30 to 40 minutes longer, until juices bubble and topping is crisp and golden. Transfer to wire rack to cool.

TIP

Always refrigerate apples to keep them fresh and crisp.

Deep Chocolate Layer Cake with Ganache Frosting

Makes 1 cake

BATTER

3 ounces semisweet chocolate, finely chopped

1½ cups hot brewed coffee

2½ cups all-purpose flour

1½ cups unsweetened cocoa powder

2 teaspoons baking soda

¾ teaspoon baking powder

1 teaspoon salt

1½ cups buttermilk

¾ cup vegetable oil

1 teaspoon vanilla extract

3 large eggs

3 cups granulated sugar

GANACHE FROSTING

1 pound semisweet chocolate, finely chopped

1 cup heavy cream

1 tablespoon corn syrup

4 tablespoons (½ stick) unsalted butter, diced

Make this cake for a very special occasion. Use the best chocolate you can find for the deepest chocolate flavor.

1. Preheat oven to 350°F. Lightly butter two 10-inch cake pans; line pan bottoms with rounds of parchment or wax paper. Lightly butter paper.
2. In a small bowl, combine chopped chocolate and hot coffee. Let sit until chocolate melts, stirring occasionally.
3. For batter: Set a sifter over a large bowl. Sift flour, cocoa powder, baking soda, baking powder and salt. In glass measuring cup, combine buttermilk, oil and vanilla.
4. In a large bowl with electric mixer on high speed, beat eggs and sugar until light and thickened, about 5 minutes. Beat in melted chocolate mixture until blended. Alternately add buttermilk mixture and dry ingredients; beat until just combined.
5. Pour batter evenly into prepared pans. Bake 1 hour, until a toothpick inserted in center comes out clean. Transfer pans to wire racks; let cool at least 30 minutes. Run a knife around edges to release from pan; invert layers onto racks. Remove paper and cool completely.
6. For frosting: Place chopped chocolate in a medium bowl. In a small saucepan over low heat, bring cream and corn syrup just to a boil, whisking often. Remove from heat; immediately pour over chocolate. Whisk in diced butter until smooth. Let frosting cool, stirring occasionally, until it is of spreading consistency. (This may take several hours, depending on kitchen temperature. Refrigerate if needed.) Frost cake as desired.

TIP

The layers can be baked one day in advance, wrapped in plastic and stored at room temperature.

Oatmeal Date Bars

T his homey bar cookie is a perfect partner for a cup of tea.

1. Preheat oven to 350°F. Line a 9-by-13-inch baking pan with foil, overhanging edges to serve as handles. Lightly coat foil with cooking spray.
2. In a large bowl with electric mixer on high speed, beat butter and both sugars about 3 minutes, until light and fluffy. Beat in eggs and vanilla.
3. In a medium bowl, combine flour, salt, baking powder and cinnamon. Fold dry ingredients into butter mixture. Stir in oats, dates and walnuts.
4. Spread batter into prepared pan. Bake 25 minutes. Halfway during baking, turn baking pan from front to back. Do not overbake. Bars will still be a bit soft and not brown. Transfer to wire rack to cool. Use foil edges to lift bars out of pan and cut into squares.

Makes 24 servings

1 cup (2 sticks) unsalted butter, at room temperature, plus extra for pan

1 cup light brown sugar

1 cup granulated sugar

2 large eggs

1 teaspoon vanilla extract

1½ cups all-purpose flour

½ teaspoon salt

½ teaspoon baking powder

½ teaspoon ground cinnamon

3 cups old-fashioned or quick oats

2 cups chopped dates

1½ cups toasted chopped walnuts

These are Mack's favorites. I wonder if Corrie will share the recipe with Mary Jo Wyse.

TIP

Chopping dates can be a sticky mess. Make the task easier by storing pitted dates in the freezer. Not only will they keep for months, they will be much easier to chop.

Golden Toffee Blondies

Makes 24 servings

1 cup (2 sticks) unsalted butter, plus extra for pan

1¾ cups light brown sugar

2 large eggs

2 teaspoons vanilla extract

2 cups all-purpose flour

½ teaspoon salt

1 12-ounce package semisweet chocolate chips

1 cup toffee bits (such as Heath)

TIP

The key to moist blondies is making sure you don't overbake them. The top of the bars should be shiny, yet the middle of the bars will still feel soft to the touch.

Perfect for bake sales or afterschool snacks, these bars are in the oven in just 10 minutes.

1. Preheat oven to 350°F. Position rack to upper third of oven. Line a 9-by-13-inch baking pan with a large sheet of foil, pressing foil so that it fits snugly into corners of the pan and overhanging edges serve as handles. Lightly butter foil.

2. In a glass measuring cup, microwave butter until melted. In large bowl with electric mixer, beat melted butter with sugar about 1 minute. Add eggs and vanilla; beat until combined and light in color. Add flour and salt and beat until just combined. Fold in chocolate chips and toffee bits.

3. Pour batter into prepared pan. Bake 25 minutes. Blondies will be golden brown on the edges yet still soft in the middle. Do not overbake. Transfer to wire rack to cool. When completely cool, use foil edges to lift blondies out of pan and cut into squares.

To my way of thinking, the gooier these are the better. Grace agrees with me.

Apple-Date Torte

Makes 1 cake

3 apples, peeled, cored and sliced (about 3 cups)

¾ cup plus 2 tablespoons granulated sugar

2 teaspoons ground cinnamon

12 tablespoons (1½ sticks) unsalted butter, plus extra for pan

2 large eggs, lightly beaten

1 cup all-purpose flour

Pinch salt

3 dates, pitted and sliced lengthwise

Confectioners' sugar

TIP

Refrigerate fresh dates in a plastic bag for up to 2 weeks, or freeze for up to a year.

Sweet and simple, this cake is best served warm.

1. Preheat oven to 350°F. Butter a 9-inch springform pan.
2. In a medium bowl, toss apple slices with 2 tablespoons granulated sugar and cinnamon. Spread in prepared pan.
3. Melt butter in microwave. In a medium bowl, stir butter, ¾ cup granulated sugar and eggs until blended. Fold in flour and salt.
4. Spoon batter evenly over apples in pan. Arrange date slices in a circle in the center. Bake 40 minutes, until a toothpick inserted in center comes out with a few moist crumbs clinging to it. Transfer to wire rack to cool. Run a knife around edges to release from pan. Release pan sides. Sprinkle with confectioners' sugar.

I love dates, unlike Jack who claims they're a creation of the devil.

Milky Way Tart

Just like a fancy candy bar—a layer of fluffy chocolate mousse sits atop a layer of creamy caramel. Be sure to let the tart warm a bit before serving, or the caramel will be too hard to cut.

1. For crust: Preheat oven to 350°F. Pulse cookies in food processor until finely chopped. Add melted butter; pulse until fine crumbs form. Press crumbs into a 9-inch pie dish. Bake 8 minutes, until firm. Transfer to wire rack to cool.

2. For mousse: Place chocolate in a medium bowl. Bring whole milk to a simmer in a saucepan over low heat. Pour hot milk over chocolate; whisk until chocolate melts and mixture is smooth. Cool to room temperature.

3. In a large bowl, beat cream with electric mixer on high speed until soft peaks form. Gently fold whipped cream into chocolate mixture. Refrigerate until set, about 1 hour.

4. For caramel: Combine sugar and ¼ cup water in a heavy medium-sized saucepan. Stir over medium-low heat until sugar dissolves. Increase heat to high; boil without stirring about 8 minutes, until mixture is deep amber and a candy thermometer inserted in mixture reaches 350°F. Pick up the pan and swirl the mixture occasionally, but do not stir. Remove from heat; carefully add cream (mixture will bubble). Stir in the 4 tablespoons butter and salt until caramel is smooth. Pour into a 2-cup glass measuring cup. Cool 10 minutes. Pour warm caramel into crust. Refrigerate until completely cool, about 45 minutes.

5. Spoon chocolate mousse over top of caramel. Using a pastry bag or small spoon, drizzle melted chocolate in stripes over tart. Store in refrigerator; let sit at room temperature at least 20 minutes before serving.

Makes 1 9" tart

CRUST

1 9-ounce box chocolate wafer cookies (such as Nabisco)

5 tablespoons unsalted butter, melted

MOUSSE

4 ounces semisweet chocolate, finely chopped

⅓ cup whole milk

½ cup heavy cream

CARAMEL FILLING

1 cup granulated sugar

¼ cup water

¼ cup heavy cream

4 tablespoons (½ stick) unsalted butter, cut into 4 pieces

Pinch salt

1 ounce semisweet chocolate, melted, for decoration

TIP

You must use a candy thermometer when making caramel. Once the temperature reaches 350°F, immediately remove the pan from the heat and add the cream and butter to thin the caramel.

Russian Tea Cakes

These elegant cookies will keep for a week in an airtight container.

Makes 36

1. Sift flour and salt into a bowl. In a separate large bowl, with an electric mixer on high speed, beat butter until light and fluffy. Gradually add sugar and beat until blended. Add vanilla. Slowly beat in dry ingredients and pecans until combined. Refrigerate at least 1 hour or up to 1 day.

2. Preheat oven to 400°F. Form dough into 1-inch balls. Place balls 1 inch apart on ungreased baking sheets. Bake 15 minutes, until just firm to touch. Transfer to wire rack; cool 5 minutes. Roll warm cookies in confectioners' sugar. Cool completely. Roll cooled cookies in confectioners' sugar again. Store in airtight container.

2 cups all-purpose flour

¼ teaspoon salt

1 cup (2 sticks) unsalted butter, room temperature

2 cups confectioners' sugar, plus extra for rolling

2 teaspoons vanilla extract

1 cup pecans, toasted and finely chopped

TIP

Keep an eye on the cookies in the oven since they don't really change color as they bake. Cookies are done when they feel firm to the touch.

I believe the Cold War would've ended years sooner if the Russians had served these at peace talks.

Orange Bundt Cake

Makes 1 cake

This moist orange-scented pound cake is a delicious change of pace. Serve with a dollop of whipped cream or dark chocolate ice cream.

CAKE

1½ cups granulated sugar

1½ cups cake flour (not self-rising)

2 teaspoons baking powder

½ teaspoon salt

7 large eggs, divided

2 tablespoons grated orange zest and ¾ cup freshly squeezed orange juice (from 2 oranges)

½ cup vegetable oil

1½ teaspoons vanilla extract

Pinch cream of tartar

GLAZE

4 tablespoons (½ stick) unsalted butter, melted

¼ cup orange juice

2 cups sifted confectioners' sugar

1. Preheat oven to 325°F; set oven rack to lower-middle position. Butter a large Bundt pan and lightly dust with flour.
2. For batter: In a large bowl, whisk sugar, flour, baking powder and salt until combined. Whisk in two whole eggs, five egg yolks (reserve whites), orange zest and juice, oil and vanilla until batter is just smooth.
3. In a large bowl with electric mixer on high speed, beat reserved egg whites about 1 minute, until foamy. Add cream of tartar, decrease speed to medium-high, and beat until thick and stiff, almost dry. (Depending on the mixer used, this will take from 5 to 10 minutes.) With large rubber spatula, fold whites into batter until completely blended.
4. Pour batter into prepared pan. Bake 55 to 60 minutes, until toothpick inserted in center comes out clean. Transfer to wire rack; let cool at least 30 minutes. Run a knife around the edges of the pan; turn out onto wire rack to cool completely.
5. For glaze: In a medium bowl, whisk butter, orange juice and confectioners' sugar until smooth. Let glaze stand 2 minutes to set. Slowly drizzle glaze over cake, letting excess slide down sides. If glaze is too thick, stir in additional 1 tablespoon orange juice. Let cake stand until glaze dries, about 30 minutes.

TIP

For a completely smooth glaze, be sure to sift the confectioners' sugar.

Three-Minute Chocolate Sauce

This super-rich sauce makes a great holiday gift. To serve, set jar in a pot of simmering water just until warm, or warm the sauce in the microwave. Don't let it come to a simmer.

1. Combine all ingredients in a microwave-safe medium bowl and place in microwave. Heat for 1 minute; stir. Heat for another minute; stir. Heat for 30 seconds; stir. Chocolate should be almost melted. Remove from microwave; continue stirring until completely melted and smooth.
2. Pour into a glass jar or several small jars. Store in the refrigerator.

Makes 2½ cups

1 12-ounce bag semisweet chocolate chips

¾ cup heavy cream

¼ cup strong brewed coffee

¼ cup confectioners' sugar

1 teaspoon vanilla extract

½ teaspoon salt

TIP

Store the sauce, tightly sealed, in the refrigerator, where it will keep for months.

Three minutes never seems as long as when you're waiting for this chocolate sauce.

Double Ginger Cake with Lemon Drizzle

Dark, moist and spicy, this cake makes a dazzling dessert for a holiday party. Since the cake is sturdy enough to transport, volunteer to bring it to your next winter gathering. And prepare to receive compliments!

1. Preheat oven to 350°F. Butter a large (10-cup) tube pan; lightly dust with flour.

2. For batter: In a large bowl, whisk flour, ground ginger, baking soda, cinnamon, cloves, allspice and salt until combined. In a large bowl with electric mixer on high speed, beat butter and brown sugar until creamy. Add eggs; beat until combined. Pour in molasses and boiling water; beat until blended. Fold in dry ingredients just until blended.

3. Pour batter into prepared pan. Bake 1 hour and 10 minutes, until a toothpick inserted in center comes out clean. Transfer to wire rack; let cool at least 30 minutes. Run a knife carefully around the edges of the pan; turn out on wire rack to cool completely.

4. For glaze: In medium bowl, whisk confectioners' sugar, cream and lemon juice. Add more juice if needed to reach drizzling consistency. Drizzle over cooled cake. Sprinkle with crystallized ginger or lemon zest.

TIP

Look for crystallized ginger in the spice section of your supermarket. Can't find it? It's fine to leave it out.

Makes 12 servings

CAKE

3½ cups all-purpose flour

1 tablespoon plus 2 teaspoons ground ginger

2 teaspoons baking soda

½ teaspoon ground cinnamon

¼ teaspoon ground cloves

¼ teaspoon allspice

½ teaspoon salt

1 cup (2 sticks) unsalted butter, at room temperature, plus more for pan

1¼ cups brown sugar

2 large eggs

2 cups molasses

1 cup boiling water

GLAZE

1 cup sifted confectioners' sugar

1 tablespoon heavy cream

2 tablespoons fresh lemon juice, or more as needed

½ cup chopped crystallized ginger or 2 tablespoons lemon zest, for garnish

Easter

at **15 EAGLE CREST AVENUE** *with*

Ben and Charlotte Rhodes

I so love Easter and the fresh promise of spring. My husband, Clyde, and I used to put on an annual Easter egg hunt for the grandchildren. How he loved painting the eggs and coming up with inventive places to hide them. Unfortunately he died when they were still young. One of their most treasured memories of their grandfather is those Easter egg hunts.

Now Olivia and Jack have started an Easter egg hunt for *their* grandchildren. I was there for the first one last year and relived so many wonderful Easter Sundays from the past.

Of course, this holiday isn't really about finding eggs and baskets filled with chocolate bunnies, but those activities do help a child understand the significance of Easter. It's so appropriate that this momentous spiritual occasion is celebrated in spring, the season of renewal.

Many families have their own distinctive ways of marking this important feast day. I've told you about ours, which also includes a dinner with dishes I serve year after year. Every

recipe here has a tradition behind it. The recipe for Cheddar Biscuits is one passed down to me by Clyde's mother. She said it was one of her family's favorite Easter treats and it became ours, too.

I first came across the Sweet and Spicy Baked Ham in Savannah, Georgia. Years ago Clyde had an opportunity to travel there for his job with the Bremerton shipyard and I was able to accompany him. One night we had dinner in a delightful old inn, and he ordered the ham. Neither of us had ever had anything like it before. Clyde enjoyed it immensely and talked so lovingly about that ham that I had to create my own version. He was more than happy to test each attempt until we arrived at the one I've included here. I can assure you it has his personal stamp of approval. Now, after so many years, Easter just wouldn't feel right without this delicious baked ham.

Another family favorite that automatically goes with our Easter celebration is Deviled Eggs, although when Will and Olivia were small they insisted on calling them angel eggs instead. They're ideal for brunch or as an appetizer before the meal.

After church and the Easter egg hunt and then our family dinner—followed by my Easter Bunny Cake—Clyde would read the Easter story to our children and, later, grandchildren. I can picture them gathered around him and I can still hear his deep, resonant voice as he read from his Bible. I didn't think I'd survive after I lost him but, as every widow does, I learned that life goes on.

Finding love again after twenty years came as a wonderful surprise. I agree with the sentiment on a friend's T-shirt—getting old isn't for sissies—but I can't help feeling that the best is yet to come for Ben and me. We're forging traditions of our own.

My wish is that you'll establish Easter traditions for your family, too. Perhaps you already have, and if that's the case I hope you'll continue them. If you find an Easter recipe or two among the ones I've collected here, I'll feel as though I'm part of your family—and you're part of mine.

Deviled Eggs for Angels

Makes 12

6 hard-boiled eggs

2 tablespoons mayonnaise

1 tablespoon extra-virgin olive oil

1 teaspoon Dijon mustard

2 tablespoons minced celery, plus additional for garnish

1 tablespoon chopped fresh tarragon

1 teaspoon minced drained capers, if desired

Salt and pepper, to taste

TIP

For ease in peeling, plunge the eggs in ice-cold water directly after cooking. Start peeling the egg at the rounded end, where there is an air bubble.

For a fun variation on this classic party dish, fold in ¼ cup chopped, cooked shrimp.

1. Peel eggs; halve lengthwise. Transfer yolks to a small bowl and mash with fork. Set aside whites. Add mayonnaise, oil and mustard to yolks. Stir in minced celery, tarragon and capers. Season to taste with +salt and pepper.

2. Using an iced teaspoon, fill egg whites with yolk mixture. Sprinkle with additional finely minced celery.

Cheddar Biscuits

Bake these tender biscuits immediately after cutting them; if you allow them to sit for any length of time, they won't rise properly in the oven.

1. Preheat oven to 425°F; set oven rack to upper-middle position. Line a baking sheet with parchment paper.
2. In a medium bowl, whisk flour, cheese, sugar, baking powder and salt. Stir in cream with a wooden spoon until dough forms.
3. Transfer dough to a lightly floured countertop. Shape dough into a round disk about ¾-inch thick. Cut into rounds with a biscuit cutter and place on prepared sheet. Combine any scraps, reroll and cut out rest. Brush rounds with melted butter and sprinkle with a little more grated cheese if desired. Bake 16 minutes, or until golden brown, rotating baking sheet halfway through baking.

Makes about 10

2 cups all-purpose flour

½ cup shredded sharp cheddar cheese, plus more for garnish

2 teaspoons granulated sugar

2 teaspoons baking powder

½ teaspoon salt

1¼ cups heavy cream

2 tablespoons unsalted butter, melted

TIP

Increase the cheese flavor by sprinkling the biscuits with additional shredded cheese before baking.

Olivia has always been a picky eater. But not when it comes to these biscuits.

Asparagus Frittata

Serves 8

8 large eggs

2 tablespoons heavy cream

Salt and pepper, to taste

2 tablespoons unsalted butter

2 leeks, thinly sliced and well rinsed

1 bunch asparagus (about 1 pound), trimmed and cut into ½-inch long slices

4 ounces Fontina or Jarlsberg cheese, cut into small cubes (about 1 cup)

TIP

Broiling times can vary greatly depending on the oven used, so keep a close eye on the frittata under the heat source.

Frittatas are perfect party food, since they can be made ahead and served warm or at room temperature.

1. Preheat broiler. In medium bowl, whisk eggs, cream, salt and pepper.
2. Melt butter in a 10-inch nonstick ovenproof skillet. Add leeks; cook 4 minutes, until softened, stirring often. Add asparagus; cook 4 minutes, until tender, stirring. Pour the egg mixture over the vegetables in the pan. Cook 3 minutes, until the eggs start to set. Sprinkle on the cheese. Reduce heat to medium-low; cook 6 minutes. The frittata will be almost set, but the top will still be runny.
3. Place skillet under the broiler. Broil 4 minutes, until top is set and golden.
4. Run a spatula around the edges of the skillet to loosen the frittata. Slide the frittata onto the platter, cheese-side up.

This is a delicious way to introduce asparagus to children.

Baby Spinach Salad with Shallot Vinaigrette and Toasted Walnuts

Serves 8

1 small shallot, minced

2 tablespoons white-wine vinegar

2 teaspoons Dijon mustard

Salt and pepper, to taste

6 tablespoons extra-virgin olive oil

10 cups baby spinach (about 12 ounces)

1 pint cherry tomatoes, quartered

⅔ cup toasted walnuts, chopped

TIP

If you can't find baby spinach, substitute baby romaine or spring greens—regular spinach is too tough for this salad.

 hallots, a very mild onion, add punch to the dressing for this dark green salad. Toasted walnuts add crunch.

1. In a large serving bowl, whisk shallot, vinegar, mustard, salt and pepper until blended. Add oil in a steady stream, whisking to blend well.
2. Add spinach, tomatoes and walnuts; toss to coat.

Creamy Potato Salad

Since you can make potato salad a day ahead, it's perfect party food. Drizzling the still-warm potatoes with a mixture of pickle juice and vinegar adds a flavor punch to the spuds. Let the salad stand at room temperature for about 1 hour before serving.

1. Place potatoes in a large saucepan and add salted water to cover by 1 inch. Bring to boil over high heat; reduce heat and simmer about 8 minutes, until potatoes are tender.
2. Drain potatoes and transfer to a large bowl. Fold in pickle juice and vinegar to coat potatoes. Let sit until just warm, about 30 minutes.
3. In a large serving bowl, combine mayonnaise, powdered mustard and celery seed. Add cooled potatoes; toss to coat. Fold in celery, pickle relish and onions, and season with salt and pepper. Cover with plastic wrap and refrigerate until chilled. Gently fold in diced eggs just before serving. Garnish with parsley and paprika.

Ben likes his potato salad served at breakfast with fried eggs. Now it's a hit with the entire family.

Serves 10

3½ pounds Yukon Gold or boiling potatoes, peeled and cut into ¾-inch cubes

2 tablespoons pickle juice (from pickle relish jar)

2 tablespoons distilled white vinegar

2 cups mayonnaise

1 tablespoon powdered mustard

¼ teaspoon celery seed

3 stalks celery, finely chopped

¼ cup sweet pickle relish

¼ cup finely chopped red onions

Salt and pepper, to taste

6 hard-boiled eggs, cut into small cubes

½ cup chopped fresh parsley

Ground paprika

TIP

Use firm-textured Yukon Gold potatoes. They hold their shape after cooking and won't turn mushy in a salad.

Colorful Fruit Salad with Vanilla-Lime Yogurt

A cheery fruit salad is a welcome addition to any holiday table, especially if kids are included.

1. In a large serving bowl, toss all the berries, pineapple and grapes with 1 tablespoon of the lime juice.
2. In a small pitcher, combine yogurt with remaining 1 tablespoon juice and zest. Serve yogurt dressing on the side for drizzling over the fruit salad.

Serves 8

1 pint fresh raspberries

1 pint fresh strawberries, hulled and quartered

1 pint fresh blueberries

1 cup fresh pineapple chunks

1 cup halved green grapes

Zest and juice from 1 lime (about 1 teaspoon zest and 2 tablespoons juice)

2 6-ounce containers vanilla yogurt (1½ cups)

This is a wonderful salad any time of year. When Justine was little, she used to pick out all the blueberries and eat them.

TIP

Remember to zest the limes before juicing them.

Sweet and Spicy Baked Ham

Serves 8 to 10

1 fully-cooked bone-in ham with rind (about 7 pounds)

1 cup apple cider

½ cup Dijon mustard

1 cup brown sugar

2 teaspoons freshly ground pepper

TIP

Select a bone-in ham for best flavor. Avoid packages labeled "Ham and water product."

Since smoked hams are fully cooked, here you are just warming the meat and adding a delicious sweet and savory crust.

1. Preheat oven to 350°F. Line a large roasting pan with heavy-duty foil. Place ham on a rack in a large roasting pan. Trim any tough rind and fat from upper side of ham, leaving ¼-inch-thick layer of fat. Using long sharp knife, score fat in 1-inch-wide diamond pattern. Place ham in prepared pan. Pour cider over ham, coating as much of the ham as possible. Cover ham and roasting pan completely with heavy-duty foil, sealing tightly at edges of pan. Bake ham 1½ hours. Remove from oven. Increase oven temperature to 400°F.

2. Remove foil from ham. Drain and discard liquids from roasting pan. Spread mustard evenly over top and sides of ham. Pat brown sugar over mustard coating, pressing firmly to adhere. Sprinkle entire ham with pepper. Place ham back on rack in roasting pan and bake about 30 minutes, spooning any mustard and sugar glaze that slides into roasting pan back over ham.

3. Transfer ham to serving platter; let cool at least 15 minutes. Slice ham and serve warm or at room temperature.

Fancy Lemon Pound Cake with Glaze

Makes 1 loaf

CAKE

1½ cups cake flour
(not self-rising)

1 teaspoon baking powder

½ teaspoon salt

1½ cups granulated sugar

2 tablespoons lemon zest

2 teaspoons fresh lemon juice

4 large eggs

2 teaspoons vanilla extract

1 cup unsalted butter (2 sticks),
melted, plus extra for greasing
the pan

GLAZE

2 tablespoons melted butter

2 tablespoons fresh lemon juice

1 cup confectioners' sugar

This moist cake makes an elegant ending to any springtime dinner party. Omit the glaze for a fantastic brunch treat.

1. Preheat oven to 350°F; set oven rack to middle position. Lightly butter and flour a 9-by-5-inch loaf pan.
2. For batter: In a medium bowl, whisk flour, baking powder and salt.
3. In food processor, pulse granulated sugar and zest until combined. Add lemon juice, eggs and vanilla; process until combined. With machine running, add 1 cup melted butter in steady stream. Transfer mixture to a large bowl. Fold in flour mixture until just combined.
4. Pour batter into prepared pan; smooth top. Bake 60 to 70 minutes, until golden brown and a toothpick inserted in the center comes out clean. Transfer to a wire rack; cool in pan 15 minutes. Run a knife around pan edges; invert cake onto rack. Turn cake right-side up and cool completely.
5. For glaze: In a small bowl, whisk 2 tablespoons melted butter, 2 tablespoons lemon juice and confectioners' sugar until smooth. Drizzle over cooled cake.

TIP

Always use pure vanilla extract, which has a far superior flavor to imitation vanilla.

Easter Bunny Cake

Serves 10 to 12

Although you can buy a pan shaped like a bunny, you can also create a perfectly cute bunny using two 9-inch cake pans. Kids can join in the fun by decorating the cake with jelly beans for eyes and nose and licorice for whiskers.

1. Preheat oven to 325°F. Lightly butter two 9-inch cake pans. Line pan bottoms with parchment or wax paper; butter paper.
2. For batter: In a medium bowl, combine flour, baking powder, baking soda, salt and cinnamon until combined. In a large bowl with electric mixer, beat granulated sugar, oil and vanilla until blended. Add eggs, one at a time, beating well after each addition. Slowly add dry ingredients, beating just until blended.
3. Fold carrots, pecans and coconut into batter until combined. Spread batter into prepared pans, smoothing top. Bake 50 to 55 minutes, until toothpick inserted in center comes out clean. Transfer to wire rack; cool for 15 minutes. Run a knife around edges of cake to loosen from pan; invert onto wire rack to cool completely. Remove wax paper.
4. For frosting: In a large bowl with electric mixer on medium speed, beat cream cheese, butter and vanilla until smooth and completely blended, about 2 minutes. Slowly add confectioners' sugar, beating until smooth. Increase speed and beat 2 minutes until frosting reaches spreading consistency.
5. Place one cooled cake at the bottom of a large platter or foil-lined rectangle of cardboard. Place the other cake on a cutting board. Cut two long oval-shaped bunny ears out of the cake on the cutting board. Place the ears above the cake on the platter. (Reserve or eat the scraps.) Frost the bunny cake. Decorate as desired. (You can also cover the entire cake with additional shredded coconut before adding a bunny face.)

CAKE

2 cups all-purpose flour

2 teaspoons baking powder

2 teaspoons baking soda

1 teaspoon salt

2 teaspoons ground cinnamon

2 cups granulated sugar

1¼ cups vegetable oil

1 tablespoon vanilla extract

4 large eggs

3 cups grated peeled carrots (from about ¾ pound carrots)

1 cup chopped pecans

1 cup sweetened coconut flakes

FROSTING

8 ounces cream cheese, at room temperature

½ cup (1 stick) unsalted butter, at room temperature

1 teaspoon vanilla extract

2½ cups sifted confectioners' sugar

TIP

You can also assemble the cake in the traditional layer-cake shape. Either way, you'll have enough frosting.

Fourth of July

at 92 PACIFIC BOULEVARD and
THE WATERFRONT PARK with

Troy and Faith Davis

I love birthdays, always have. Faith Davis (who used to be Faith Beckwith) feels the same way. She's so good about remembering everyone's birthday and now that she and Troy are married, there are a lot more of them to celebrate. One that's especially fun for both of us is the Fourth of July— a birthday the entire country celebrates.

Harry, my cat, hates all the noise and the fireworks, but I keep him securely inside the house. Justine says it's the same with their dog, Penny, who cowers upstairs under one of the beds. Harry, being a cat, has more dignity but seems to think I'm doing this to him on purpose. However, Harry and Penny are the *only* members of the family who voice any objections to our Fourth of July celebrations.

Believe me when I tell you that no one complains about the community barbecue!

Faith has just begun a new tradition for our Fourth of July celebration. We start with a light brunch at 92 Pacific Boulevard. Not everyone comes to that, of course, just eight or ten of us, but after the meal we help Faith in her kitchen, marinating chicken pieces and making vats of potato salad. Then we head out to the Waterfront Park.

The entire community of Cedar Cove is invited to join in a potluck picnic down at the park, and we all bring our special Fourth of July dishes. Faith doesn't

dare show up without her marinated chicken. Troy, Bob Beldon and a few other husbands man the barbecues, and the aroma drifts through the park until all our mouths are watering.

Everyone always asks for my Herb Garden Pesto Rigatoni, too. Peggy's presence (and Bob's, of course!) is eagerly anticipated—and it isn't just because of her Strawberry-Rhubarb Crisp. That's another one of those recipes in high demand. No one makes it better than Peggy and I suspect it's because she grows both in her large garden.

Corrie contributes a dessert, too. She usually brings a Peach and Raspberry Cobbler and has always refused to share the recipe—until now. To be fair, she didn't *refuse* to share, she just kept forgetting…or so she says. We love to tease her about that.

Olivia's contribution is her Grilled Baguette and Tomato Salad, which is just perfect for summer.

We arrive at the park shortly after twelve and have everything set up and ready by midafternoon. For the last few years the men (and a few of the women) have gotten involved in a poker tournament spearheaded by Jack. The rest of us generally just visit in that wonderful way women do. It makes for such a relaxing afternoon and such a great opportunity to catch up on gossip. (Oops! I mean *news*.) Naturally I work on my knitting, and I'm not the only one. Faith and, more recently Troy's daughter, Megan, also bring theirs.

There's always food left over for a late-evening snack, so we bring everything out again before the fireworks. And last year there were some private fireworks, too—I saw Troy and Faith cuddling in the dark. I do love a romance; I think everyone does. All I can say is that it took them long enough to realize what most of us already knew. Troy and Faith belong together. I'm so glad they were willing to put their differences behind them. I know Megan agrees with me, as do Scott and Jay Lynn, Faith's children.

We have a lot to celebrate in our community and our country. The Fourth of July represents the triumphs of the past and all our hopes for the future. I can't think of a more appropriate way to spend it than with family, good friends and good food.

Fresh Summer Salsa with Homemade Tortilla Chips

Makes 48 tortilla chips and 2 cups salsa

CHIPS

6 medium flour tortillas

Olive oil

Kosher or sea salt, to taste

SALSA

3 large tomatoes (about 2 pounds), cut into small dice and drained of juice

1 red bell pepper

1 jalapeño pepper, seeded and minced

¼ small red onion, cut into small dice

2 cloves garlic, minced

2 tablespoons fresh lime juice (from 1 lime)

2 tablespoons cider vinegar

¼ teaspoon ground cumin

¼ cup fresh cilantro, chopped

This is a mild salsa; add another jalapeño or extra hot sauce if you want it spicier.

1. For tortilla chips: Preheat oven to 300°F. Stack tortillas and cut stack into eight wedges. (You'll have 48.) Arrange wedges on a baking sheet. Brush with oil; sprinkle with salt. Bake 12 minutes, or until golden. Transfer to a wire rack to cool.
2. For salsa: Combine all ingredients except cilantro in a large bowl. Add cilantro just before serving.

Most of these ingredients come straight from my garden or from the Farmer's Market. I like my salsa with lots of garlic.

TIP

Don't let homemade salsa sit for more than 4 hours at room temperature. The texture will soften too much and the bright flavor will dull. You can cover it tightly with plastic wrap and store in the refrigerator for up to 3 days, but it's always best eaten freshly made.

Creamy Bean Dip

start to finish, it takes about 5 minutes to get this dip in the oven, so you don't need to make it in advance.

1. Preheat oven to 350°F. In a large bowl, blend beans, cream cheese, sour cream and seasoning mix. Fold in cheese cubes.
2. Scoop dip into a 2-quart casserole. Bake 30 minutes, until cheese melts and dip is warmed through.

Makes about 6 cups

1 15-ounce can refried beans

4 ounces cream cheese, at room temperature

1 cup sour cream

1 package taco seasoning mix

½ pound Velveeta or sharp cheddar cheese, cut into cubes

TIP

If you want to shave a few more moments off the already-quick preparation time, use preshredded cheese.

Grilled Baguette and Tomato Salad

Don't refrigerate this salad; the bread will get too soggy and tomatoes will lose their flavor.

1. Split bread horizontally; use ¼ cup of the olive oil to brush each piece on both sides. Grill or toast in toaster oven, until lightly charred, flipping bread to brown both sides.
2. Meanwhile, in a large bowl, combine the remaining oil, vinegar, lime juice, tomatoes, garlic, parsley, onion, salt and pepper.
3. Cut toasted bread into one-inch cubes; toss with tomato mixture. Let stand 20 minutes, to combine flavors, before serving.

Jack and Troy Davis can't get enough of this salad. It's quite humorous to watch them squabble over the last serving.

Serves 4 to 6

½ French baguette or Italian loaf

½ cup extra-virgin olive oil, divided

⅓ cup rice vinegar

2 tablespoons lime juice (from 1 lime)

3 large tomatoes (about 2 pounds), chopped

3 cloves garlic, minced

½ cup chopped fresh parsley

¼ cup chopped red onion

Salt and pepper, to taste

> **TIP**
>
> If possible, plan ahead so that this salad rests for about 20 minutes before you eat it. That lets the baguette absorb just enough of the tasty juices to be perfect for serving.

Cured Grilled Salmon with Lime-Jalapeño Butter

Serves 4

SALMON

½ cup brown sugar

¼ cup kosher salt

1 tablespoon pepper

4 salmon fillets
(about 4 ounces each)

LIME-JALAPEÑO BUTTER

½ cup (1 stick) unsalted butter,
softened

1 tablespoon chopped fresh
cilantro

1 tablespoon chopped, seeded
fresh jalapeño pepper

1 tablespoon fresh lime juice

TIP

Whenever you cook salmon,
throw a couple extra fillets on
the grill. Leftovers make a great
lunch or addition to a salad.

A roll of chili-spiked butter is an easy and impressive addition to glazed salmon. Make the flavored butter up to 2 days in advance.

1. For salmon: In a large bowl, stir brown sugar, salt and pepper until combined. Add fillets to bowl; turn to coat. Cover bowl and refrigerate 4 hours.
2. In a small bowl, stir butter, cilantro, jalapeño and lime juice until blended. Scrape mixture onto a sheet of plastic wrap; roll into a cylinder, wrapping log completely. Chill for 20 minutes, until hard enough to hold its shape.
3. Preheat grill; lightly oil grates. Grill salmon over medium heat about 4 minutes per side. Remove from grill.
4. Slice cold lime-jalapeño butter into disks. Top warm fish with flavored butter disks.

Hearty Skillet Cornbread with Bacon

Baking this substantial side dish in a cast-iron skillet imparts a rugged crust. Buttermilk and cheese make for a moist, tender interior.

1. Preheat oven to 375°F. Cook bacon in a 9-inch cast-iron skillet over medium heat until crisp. Remove bacon; transfer to a paper-towel-lined plate to drain. Pour off most of the fat from skillet. Set skillet over low heat; add butter to melt.

2. In a large bowl, combine flour, cornmeal, baking powder and salt. In another bowl, whisk buttermilk, oil, egg, sugar and baking soda until blended. Fold wet ingredients into dry until just combined. Do not overmix. Fold in cheese.

3. Scrape cornbread batter onto melted butter in warm skillet. Crumble bacon and sprinkle over top of batter. Place skillet in oven and bake 30 minutes, until top is golden and a toothpick inserted in center comes out with a few crumbs attached. Cool 5 minutes before cutting into wedges.

Serves 6 to 8

4 slices bacon

1 tablespoon unsalted butter

1 cup all-purpose flour

1 cup yellow cornmeal

1 tablespoon baking powder

¼ teaspoon salt

1¼ cups buttermilk

¼ cup vegetable oil

1 large egg

¼ cup brown sugar

½ teaspoon baking soda

1 cup shredded cheddar cheese

TIP

Baking the cornbread in a preheated, well-oiled skillet makes for the crispest crust.

Cliff Harding gave me this recipe. He's been known to toss in jalapeños without warning.

BBQ Chicken

Makes 1¼ cups sauce and 10 pieces chicken

1 cup ketchup

¼ cup cider vinegar

2 tablespoons molasses

1 tablespoon Dijon mustard

1 teaspoon Tabasco or hot sauce

1 whole chicken (about 4 pounds), cut into 10 pieces

Salt and pepper, to taste

TIP

To tell when the chicken is done, poke the tip of a knife into the thickest part of the breast and thigh; there should be no red or dark pink meat and the juices should run clear. An instant-read thermometer should read 160°F in the breast, 180°F in the thigh.

Cut the breast pieces in half to help them cook more evenly on the grill. Serve any leftover sauce on the side and store the remainder, tightly sealed, in the refrigerator for up to a week.

1. In a small saucepan over low heat, combine ketchup, vinegar, molasses, mustard and Tabasco or hot sauce. Cook for 3 to 5 minutes, stirring occasionally.

2. Preheat grill. Season chicken with salt and pepper. Place chicken pieces, skin-side down, over the hottest part of the grill. Cook, uncovered, about 2 minutes, until golden brown. Turn pieces and move off the direct flame to the cooler edges of the grill. Cook 15 to 20 minutes, turning and moving the chicken pieces occasionally to prevent charring and flare-ups.

3. Baste chicken with BBQ sauce in the last 5 minutes of grilling, turning the pieces so that the sauce is heated through.

This is a favorite dinner for Ben and me for concerts on the Cove.

Herb Garden Pesto Rigatoni

Serves 6

2 cups fresh spinach leaves, trimmed

2 cups fresh basil leaves

3 cloves garlic, chopped

⅔ cup extra-virgin olive oil

¼ cup pine nuts or walnuts

½ cup grated Parmesan cheese

Salt and pepper, to taste

1 pound rigatoni or tube pasta

TIP

This recipe makes enough pesto for 2 pounds of pasta, so freeze the extra sauce for another night.

Adding spinach to basil pesto keeps the sauce green and adds a blast of vitamins. More good news: this pasta is delicious warm, cold or at room temperature.

1. Place spinach, basil and garlic in food processor; process until finely chopped. Pour oil through feed tube; process 30 seconds. Add nuts, cheese, salt and pepper; process until sauce forms.
2. Cook pasta according to package directions; retain ½ cup cooking water before draining. Toss hot pasta with sauce, adding cooking water as needed.

Who knew pasta could be so good? And with the herbs and vegetables, you can feel virtuous while you eat it!

Strawberry-Rhubarb Crisp

This crisp topping is spiked with ginger for a delicious change of pace.

1. **For filling:** Preheat oven to 350°F. In a large bowl, combine rhubarb, strawberries, granulated sugar, lemon juice and 2 tablespoons flour. Pour into a 9-inch pie dish.
2. **For topping:** In food processor, pulse 1 cup flour, oats, brown sugar, cinnamon, ginger and salt until combined. Add butter pieces; pulse until dough holds together in clumps. Sprinkle topping evenly over fruit, mounding slightly in the center.
3. Bake 1 hour, until topping is lightly browned and fruit is bubbling. Let sit 10 minutes before serving.

Serves 8

FILLING

2 pounds rhubarb, cut into ½-inch pieces

½ pint fresh strawberries, quartered (about 1 cup)

¾ cup granulated sugar

2 tablespoons fresh lemon juice

2 tablespoons all-purpose flour

TOPPING

1 cup all-purpose flour

1 cup old-fashioned or quick oats

¾ cup dark brown sugar

1 teaspoon ground cinnamon

1 teaspoon ground ginger

Pinch salt

10 tablespoons (1¼ sticks) unsalted butter, cut into pieces, cold

— TIP

Rhubarb is best when it's fresh from the field in spring or summer. Hothouse rhubarb's flavor pales in comparison. Be sure to cut the rhubarb into small pieces so it cooks through.

Peach and Raspberry Cobbler

This brilliantly-colored pie stars the sweetest fruits of summer: peaches and raspberries. Serve the warm cobbler with vanilla ice cream or whipped cream.

1. Preheat oven to 400°F; set oven rack to lower-middle position.
2. For filling: In a large bowl, toss peaches and raspberries with ⅓ cup sugar; let stand for 10 minutes, tossing several times. Fold in cornstarch, lemon juice and salt. Pour into an 8-inch glass baking dish. Bake 10 minutes, until juices are bubbling.
3. For topping: In food processor, pulse 1 cup flour, ¼ cup sugar, baking powder, baking soda and salt to combine. Add butter; pulse until mixture resembles coarse meal. Pulse in yogurt until a wet, slightly sticky dough forms. (Do not overmix.)
4. Drop dough in 9 equal mounds over fruit, spacing them at least ½ inch apart. Lightly sprinkle mounds with additional sugar. Bake 18 minutes, until topping is golden and fruit is bubbling. Transfer to wire rack to cool.

My great-granddaughter thinks this is great finger food! Good thing raspberry washes out with bleach.

Serves 8

FILLING

2¼ pounds ripe peaches (about 6), peeled and cut into thick wedges

1 6-ounce carton raspberries (about ¾ cup)

⅓ cup granulated sugar

2 tablespoons cornstarch or flour

1 tablespoon fresh lemon juice

Pinch salt

TOPPING

1 cup all-purpose flour

¼ cup granulated sugar, plus additional for topping

¾ teaspoon baking powder

¼ teaspoon baking soda

¼ teaspoon salt

5 tablespoons unsalted butter, cold, cut into small chunks

⅓ cup plain yogurt or buttermilk

TIP

Don't make the biscuit dough ahead of time; if the unbaked dough is left to stand too long, the biscuits will not rise properly.

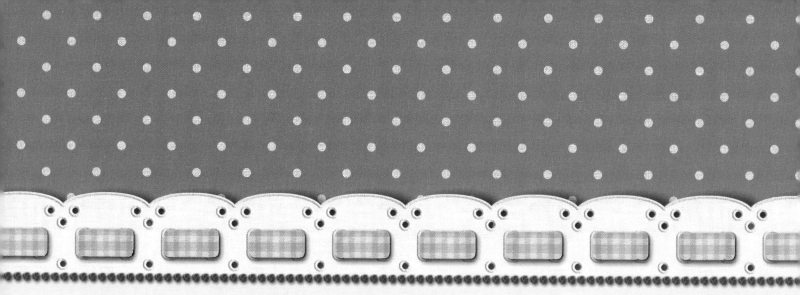

Thanksgiving

at **74 SEASIDE AVENUE** *with*

Bobby and Teri Polgar

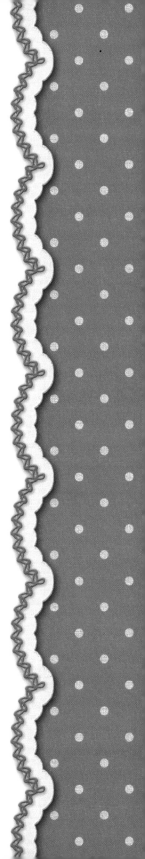

Outside of family, Bobby and Teri Polgar are two of my favorite people in Cedar Cove. Bobby is such an unconventional young man and so smart, and Teri—well, Teri is definitely her own person. She's been cutting my hair for years and I've come to appreciate her warmth and optimism. Not once in all the time I've known her has Teri hesitated to share her opinion. And she has the most unexpected sense of humor; just listening to her laugh makes me want to laugh, too.

A few years ago she made her first Thanksgiving dinner. She and Bobby hadn't been married long and she wanted this meal to be special. I was flattered that she asked my advice, although I hadn't expected her to plan the usual Thanksgiving menu, complete with turkey, stuffing, pumpkin pie and all the rest.

Naturally I was more than happy to share a few of my holiday specialties, starting with a stuffing recipe. Of all the ones I've tried—including the traditional bread stuffing—

I prefer the Rice, Sausage and Pecan version. It just doesn't seem like Thanksgiving unless I actually stuff that turkey (although some people, me included, would rather have the stuffing and gravy than the turkey itself).

Teri told me afterward that her Thanksgiving dinner turned out perfectly. Dealing with her family, however, was a disaster. If you're acquainted with her mother, who's on her fifth or sixth husband, you'll know what I'm talking about. Nevertheless, Bobby and his driver friend, James, and Teri's younger brother, Johnny, praised her dinner to the skies, and they were all the family that really mattered to Teri. Her sister, Christie, is equally important to her, of course, but I gather that Christie behaved quite badly at that dinner. Teri and Christie have had a pretty ambivalent relationship, although it appears to be improving, which is nice to hear.

When I gave her my recipes, I explained that my family's always loved the Sweet Potato Purée. I got it from my aunt Maryanne, who's been gone for many

years now. My mother wasn't fond of sweet potatoes and never made it herself, but I, on the other hand, love them. So does everyone else in my family.

Getting back to Teri, I want to tell you how impressed I am with that young woman and Bobby, too. I've never seen a husband who loves his wife more than Bobby loves Teri. I realize that sounds sentimental and perhaps excessively romantic, but I'm sincere. For most of his life, Bobby has lived and breathed chess. He's a world champion, so that's understandable. But in my opinion he didn't know what it was to love or feel loved until he met Teri. The story of how that happened always makes me smile….

Despite her disappointing Thanksgiving-dinner experience, Teri's determined to cook again. She wants to establish family traditions and since she and Bobby are about to become parents, it's a good idea to begin now. As Teri reminded me not long ago, she has much for which to be grateful. I do, too, and if we stop to think about it, we all do, one way or another. That's something we should acknowledge *every* day of the year.

So let's give thanks with humility, happiness—and a sense of fun!

Rice, Sausage and Pecan Stuffing

Serves 10 to 12

2 cups reduced-sodium chicken broth, divided

1 cup water, divided

½ cup wild rice

¾ cup long-grain white rice

3 tablespoons unsalted butter, divided

1 small onion, chopped

2 stalks celery, thinly sliced

½ pound sweet sausage, casings removed

1 tart apple, peeled and diced

½ cup dried cranberries

½ cup chopped pecans

1 teaspoon dried sage

¾ teaspoon dried whole thyme

Salt and pepper, to taste

Stick this savory fruit-and-nut-studded side dish in the oven to warm while the turkey is resting.

1. In a medium saucepan, combine 1 cup of the broth and ½ cup water; bring to a boil over high heat. Add wild rice; bring to a boil again. Reduce heat to low; cover and cook 45 to 50 minutes, until rice is tender and liquid absorbed.

2. In another medium saucepan, combine remaining 1 cup broth and ½ cup water; bring to a boil over high heat. Add white rice; bring to a boil. Reduce heat to low; cover and cook 17 minutes, until rice is tender and liquid absorbed.

3. Preheat oven to 325°F. Melt 2 tablespoons butter in a large heavy skillet over medium-low heat. Add onion and celery; cook 7 minutes, until softened, stirring. Scrape into large bowl. In same skillet over medium heat, cook sausage until no longer pink, breaking up meat clumps with the back of a wooden spoon. Drain and discard fat; add sausage to bowl with vegetables.

4. Add cooked wild and white rice to bowl with vegetables. Stir in apple, cranberries, pecans, sage, thyme, salt and pepper. Spoon into a 2-quart casserole; dot with remaining 1 tablespoon butter. Cover pan and bake 30 minutes, until warmed through.

TIP

Get a jump start on the dish by cooking the rice a day in advance.

Cranberry-Orange Relish

Grand Marnier adds elegance and a shot of extra flavor to this zesty relish. If you prefer not to use it, substitute orange juice.

1. In a heavy medium saucepan, combine sugar, water and orange juice. Bring to simmer over high heat until sugar dissolves. Add cranberries; reduce heat and cook at gentle simmer until cranberries begin to pop.
2. Remove from heat and stir in dried cranberries, Grand Marnier or orange juice, and salt. Transfer sauce to medium bowl; let cool. Cover and refrigerate until cold.

Serves 8

¾ cup granulated sugar

½ cup water

¼ cup orange juice

1 12-ounce bag fresh cranberries

⅓ cup dried cranberries

¼ cup Grand Marnier or orange juice

Pinch salt

TIP

Make the sauce up to one week in advance. Refrigerate, tightly covered.

Be sure and have extra Grand Marnier on hand. Not for the relish but for the cook.

Braised Brussels Sprouts with Bacon

The reason Brussels sprouts have a bad reputation is because they are so often overcooked. In this savory side dish, the tiny cabbages are first browned and then braised in the oven until just cooked through, which brings out their nutty flavor.

1. Preheat oven to 350°F. In large heavy skillet over medium heat, cook bacon until crisp. Using a slotted spoon, transfer to a paper-towel-lined plate. Crumble into large pieces.

2. In same skillet over medium heat, cook sprouts in bacon fat about 5 minutes, until they start to brown, shaking the pan often. Add broth (it should come about ⅓ of the way up the sides of the sprouts); bring broth to a simmer. Transfer to oven, cook 15 minutes, until sprouts are cooked but still have some bite.

3. Using a slotted spoon, transfer sprouts to a medium serving bowl, season with thyme, salt and pepper and garnish with crumbled bacon.

Serves 6 to 8

3 slices bacon, for garnish

1½ pounds Brussels sprouts, trimmed and halved if large

1 cup reduced-sodium chicken broth, or more if needed

1 teaspoon chopped fresh thyme or ½ teaspoon dried whole thyme

Salt and pepper, to taste

TIP

Test sprouts for doneness by poking one with a paring knife. The knife should slide in easily, yet with some give. The sprouts should not be soft.

I do so enjoy Brussels sprouts. I never could interest Will or Olivia in them, and that's their loss.

Sweet Potato Purée

Serves 8

**4 pounds sweet potatoes
(6 to 8 medium)**

½ cup half-and-half

**6 tablespoons unsalted butter,
cut into chunks**

1 tablespoon vanilla extract

Salt and pepper, to taste

TIP

Remember that smaller sweet
potatoes usually have sweeter
flavor than the larger ones.

Sweet potatoes are often mislabeled as yams, which is a tropical vegetable that is rarely available in the U.S. The vegetable available in your market is likely a sweet potato, no matter what the sign says.

1. Preheat oven to 400°F. Poke each sweet potato several times with a fork; bake for 45 minutes, or until tender. Cool slightly; cut in half lengthwise. Using spoon, scoop pulp into bowl of food processor. Purée until mostly smooth.

2. In a small saucepan over low heat, warm half-and-half and butter until blended. Stir in vanilla. With the processor on, carefully pour warm butter mixture into potatoes; process until smooth. Season with salt and pepper; transfer to a serving bowl.

*The words sweet and
potato say all that's
necessary regarding
this dish. Enjoy!*

Mashed Potato Casserole

Serves 6

2½ pounds russet potatoes, peeled and cut into chunks

4 ounces cream cheese, cut into chunks, softened

½ cup sour cream

¼ cup milk, heated

Salt and pepper, to taste

Chopped fresh chives, for garnish

TIP

The potatoes can be prepared up to 4 hours ahead, covered loosely with plastic wrap, and kept at room temperature. Alternatively, cool them, cover tightly with plastic wrap and refrigerate for up to 1 day.

All the deliciousness of mashed potatoes combined with the ease of a make-ahead casserole. Feel free to double the recipe and bake in two casseroles. Select high-starch spuds, such as russet or Idaho, for the best mash. They bake up fluffier than boiling varieties.

1. In a medium saucepan, cover potato chunks with salted water. Bring to a boil over high heat. Reduce the heat to medium and simmer 15 minutes, until the potatoes are tender.
2. Drain potatoes; return to the warm pot set over low heat. Add cream cheese. Using a potato masher, mash the mixture until cream cheese melts. Mash in sour cream and milk. Season with salt and pepper. Transfer to a buttered casserole. Let cool.
3. Preheat oven to 375°F. Bake casserole 30 to 40 minutes, until potatoes are warmed through. Serve hot, sprinkled with chives.

Okay, I'll confess. For Thanksgiving I add butter to this. No one's watching calories then, anyway.

Holiday Cranberry Bread

This moist loaf cake makes a wonderful not-too-sweet ending to the meal, an excellent breakfast, or an ideal hostess gift. The rosewater adds a delicate fragrance that perfectly complements the cranberries.

1. Preheat oven to 350°F. Lightly butter and flour a 9-by-5-inch loaf pan. In a medium bowl, whisk flour, baking powder, baking soda and salt.

2. In a large bowl, whisk eggs and sugar until blended. Stir in melted butter. Mix the milk with the rosewater, if using, and stir into the eggs and sugar. Fold in dry ingredients just until blended, then add the cranberries and nuts. Scrape batter into prepared pan; smooth top.

3. Bake for 55 minutes, or until toothpick inserted in center comes out clean. Transfer to wire rack; cool for 10 minutes. Run a knife around pan edges; invert cake onto wire rack. Cool completely.

Makes 1 loaf

3 cups all-purpose flour

1 teaspoon baking powder

1 teaspoon baking soda

1 teaspoon salt

2 large eggs

1¼ cups granulated sugar

4 tablespoons (½ stick) butter, melted

1¼ cups whole milk

1 teaspoon rosewater (optional)

1¼ cups fresh cranberries (about 6 ounces), roughly chopped

¾ cup chopped walnuts or pecans

TIP

Look for rosewater in the spice section of your supermarket. If unavailable, you can leave it out of the recipe.

Green Salad with Roasted Pear, Roquefort Cheese and Raspberry Vinaigrette

Pears and Roquefort are a classic salad combination, but roasting the pears and adding a raspberry vinaigrette takes this version to new heights.

1. Preheat oven to 450°F. Place a baking sheet in the oven to warm.
2. Using a paring knife, slice out the core of each pear half. Cut pear halves lengthwise into thin slices.
3. In a large bowl, toss pears with butter and sugar. Spread pears in single layer on preheated baking sheet. Roast about 10 minutes, until browned. Flip each slice and roast 5 minutes longer, until deep golden brown and tender. Let cool on baking sheet.
4. Meanwhile, in blender or food processor, blend vinegar and shallots. With machine running, gradually add oil. Season with salt and pepper.
5. In a large serving bowl, combine romaine and radicchio. Toss with enough vinaigrette to coat. Garnish salad with pears, cheese and pecans, if using.

> TIP
>
> This recipe makes more dressing than you will need. It will keep, tightly covered, for several days in the refrigerator.

Serves 8 to 10

3 firm Anjou or Bartlett pears (about 2 pounds), peeled and halved

1 tablespoon unsalted butter, melted

2 tablespoons granulated sugar

¼ cup raspberry vinegar

2 medium shallots, coarsely chopped

⅓ cup extra-virgin olive oil

Salt and pepper, to taste

1 small head romaine lettuce, thinly sliced

1 head radicchio, thinly sliced

2 ounces Roquefort or blue cheese, crumbled

½ cup toasted pecans, if desired

Golden Roast Turkey with Maple Glaze

Serves 14 to 16

1 fresh turkey, about 14 to 16 pounds, at room temperature

1 apple, quartered

1 onion, halved

3 stalks celery, cut in half

3 fresh rosemary sprigs, plus extra for garnish

Salt, to taste

½ cup (1 stick) unsalted butter

½ cup maple syrup

1 cup water

Lady apples, for garnish (optional)

TIP

For big roasts, a meat thermometer is important to determine doneness. The pop-up thermometers that come with turkeys are unreliable.

There's no mystery to roasting a moist turkey. This golden bird couldn't be easier—the maple syrup adds a beautiful burnished glaze.

1. Preheat oven to 350°F. Remove giblets and neck from turkey cavity. Wash and dry turkey.
2. Stuff turkey cavity with apple, onion, celery and rosemary; sprinkle cavity with salt. Truss bird; sprinkle generously with salt. Place on V-rack in large, heavy roasting pan.
3. In a small saucepan, warm butter and maple syrup over low heat until butter melts. Pour mixture over turkey, coating as much of the bird as you can. Add 1 cup water to bottom of roasting pan.
4. Roast turkey 10 to 12 minutes for each pound. Baste with pan juices every 20 minutes. Tent turkey with foil if skin becomes too brown. Turkey is done when an instant-read thermometer inserted into thigh registers 180°F. Breast meat should reach 170°F. Transfer turkey to cutting board. Let rest for at least 20 minutes before carving. If desired, garnish turkey platter with rosemary sprigs and lady apples.

Clyde's brother, God rest his soul, sent us maple syrup from Vermont every year for Christmas.

Chocolate Chip Pecan Pie

Makes 1 pie

1 refrigerated or frozen
pie shell, thawed

3 tablespoons unsalted butter,
cut into chunks

¾ cup brown sugar

Pinch salt

2 large eggs

½ cup light corn syrup

1 teaspoon vanilla extract

1 cup toasted chopped
pecan pieces

6 ounces semisweet
chocolate chips (1 cup)

TIP

Cooking the filling gently over
simmering water prevents the
mixture from scorching.

Serve this luscious dessert warm, with ice cream or whipped cream.

1. Partially bake the pie shell according to package directions. Transfer to wire rack.

2. Lower oven temperature to 275°F. Place butter in medium heatproof bowl; set bowl over a saucepan filled with just simmering water. Remove bowl from heat once butter is melted; whisk in sugar and salt until blended. Whisk in eggs, corn syrup and vanilla. Place bowl back over simmering water; stir until mixture is warm to the touch. (A candy thermometer should read about 130°F.) Remove from heat; stir in pecans.

3. Pour warm mixture into warm crust. Evenly sprinkle chocolate chips over filling; gently press the chocolate into the filling with the back of a spoon. Bake 50 minutes. Pie is done when center is just set. Transfer to wire rack to cool, at least 4 hours. Serve pie at room temperature or warm.

Personally, I would never use a ready-made pie shell, but don't think less of those who do.

Pumpkin Pie with Cinnamon Crust and Spiced Whipped Cream

Traditional pumpkin pie gets a family-friendly makeover with the addition of a graham-cracker crust and cinnamon-spiced whipped cream.

1. For crust: Preheat oven to 350°F; set oven rack to middle position. In food processor, pulse crackers, melted butter, granulated sugar and salt until fine crumbs form. Press mixture over bottom and up sides of a 9-inch tart pan. Bake 12 to 15 minutes, until set. Transfer to a wire rack to cool. Increase oven temperature to 375°F.
2. For filling: Whisk ingredients in large bowl. Pour into crust. Bake 45 minutes, until filling is just set. Transfer to wire rack to cool completely.
3. For cream: In a large bowl with electric mixer on high speed, beat cream, confectioners' sugar and cinnamon until it holds stiff peaks. Serve immediately with pie.

> **TIP**
>
> The easy cookie crust can be made one day ahead. The pie can be baked up to 6 hours in advance.

Makes 1 pie

CRUST

1½ cups cinnamon graham cracker crumbs (from about 12 crackers)

5 tablespoons unsalted butter, melted

1 tablespoon granulated sugar

Pinch salt

FILLING

¾ cup brown sugar

2 teaspoons ground cinnamon

½ teaspoon ground ginger

½ teaspoon nutmeg

¼ teaspoon salt

1 15-ounce can solid-pack pumpkin (not pumpkin pie mix)

1¼ cups heavy cream

2 large eggs, beaten to blend

SPICED CREAM

1 cup chilled heavy cream

¼ cup confectioners' sugar

½ teaspoon cinnamon

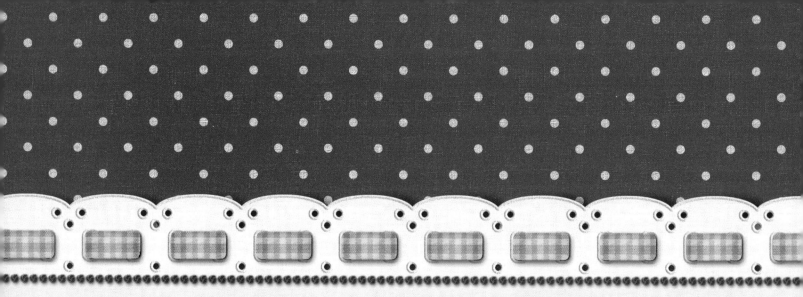

Christmas

at **8 SANDPIPER WAY** *with*

Dave and Emily Flemming

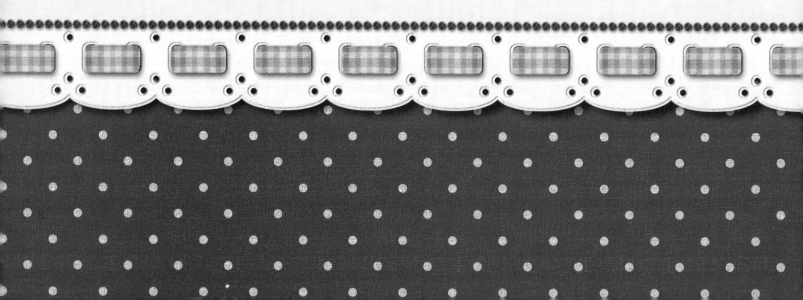

I've attended the Methodist church here in Cedar Cove for probably three decades, maybe longer. Through the years pastors have come and gone. Yet of all the ministers who've served our small congregation, none has displayed the care and godliness of Dave Flemming. He's a genuinely kind person who is truly a shepherd to his flock.

I suppose most of you heard about the scandal involving Pastor Flemming. Well, I for one refused to believe he had anything to do with that missing jewelry, and it gives me much satisfaction to say I was right. Thankfully those doubts were all laid to rest—with the help of our sheriff and our local P.I. It all happened very close to Christmas, too. What a gift for the Flemming family that Dave was so thoroughly vindicated!

And speaking of Christmas, one of the inventive ideas Pastor Flemming has brought to our church has been the annual live Nativity scene. It's a tableau featuring actors, who play all the roles from Mary and Joseph to the shepherds

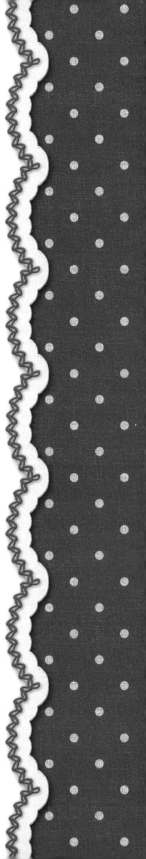

and Wise Men. And—of particular interest to the children of Cedar Cove—it includes live animals. Grace and Cliff Harding house them in their barn, which is what makes this entire project a possibility.

You've probably guessed that Christmas is my favorite holiday of the year. As much as I can, I make my own gifts; it's one small way to let others know how much I love and appreciate them. Nothing says that like a homemade gift, whether it's a knitted scarf or mittens, a tin of cookies or a fruitcake....

Dave Flemming's wife, Emily, does the same thing, although she's a quilter, not a knitter. And she's become justifiably renowned for her gift baskets of baked treats, like Sugar Cookies cut in Christmas shapes. Emily's a fine cook, too, and has a vast recipe collection. No wonder, considering all the weddings, funerals and anniversary parties she's attended! Her recipe for Beef Wellington isn't to be missed. Who knew a dish with such a fancy name could be so simple? Ever since Emily wrote out the recipe for me, Beef Wellington has become part of our family Christmas celebration, although I generally prepare it on Christmas Eve, when the whole family comes to our house.

The recipe for the Baked Potato Casserole is one of Emily's, too. That dish is, in a word, *heavenly*. Like those Super Fudge Brownies I mentioned earlier, it's best saved for special occasions. One thing's for sure: I never have to worry about leftovers and you won't, either.

A few years back, I wrote a seniors' column for *The Cedar Cove Chronicle*. Jack Griffin talked me into it, and I continued the column until my cancer scare. But now that Ben and I are married, I just don't have time anymore. I'm telling you all this because of Jack's Christmas Cookies. I happened to be at the newspaper office the day he brought them in and set them proudly on the counter, along with the recipe, which he wanted me to include in my column. I read it and laughed out loud. I can't believe he came up with this himself, although he claims he did. Jack is such a tease it's hard to know. I should tell you that this easy no-bake recipe is sure to cause lots of comment. (And I've discovered it's *perfect* for making with children!)

I just couldn't imagine Christmas without all my favorite dishes. A well-prepared meal spells love, and so does serving your family's traditional favorites. It's especially nice if other members bring or make something, too—a salad or pie, for example. Emily tells me she really enjoys sharing Christmas dinner preparations with her mom.

Don't you agree that there's no better way to celebrate Christmas than sitting at a beautifully set table, surrounded by family and friends?

Artichoke and Caramelized Onion Phyllo Pie

Serves 10 to 12

FILLING

4 tablespoons (½ stick) unsalted butter

1 small onion, thinly sliced

⅓ cup all-purpose flour

1⅔ cups whole milk

2 cups shredded Gruyère or Swiss cheese

3 cups frozen artichoke hearts (2 9-ounce packages), thawed and sliced

1 teaspoon dried whole thyme or 2 teaspoons chopped fresh thyme

Salt and pepper, to taste

CRUST

½ cup (1 stick) unsalted butter, melted

1 14-ounce box frozen phyllo pastry (about 16 sheets), thawed

Serve this rich appetizer in small slices, either warm or at room temperature. Gruyère cheese adds a more pungent flavor than Swiss.

1. For the filling: Melt 4 tablespoons butter in a medium saucepan over medium-low heat. Add onion; cook 6 minutes, until softened, stirring occasionally. Sprinkle in the flour; stirring until absorbed, about 1 minute. Gradually pour in the milk, stirring until milk is incorporated and sauce thickens. Reduce heat to low and add the cheese, stirring until it melts. Stir in artichokes, thyme, salt and pepper.

2. For the crust: Using a pastry brush, coat the bottom and sides of a 9-inch springform pan with some of the melted butter. Preheat oven to 300°F. Brush a phyllo sheet with butter and lay it in the pan, pushing down to fill the pan and draping the edges of the pastry over the sides. Brush another sheet of phyllo with butter and fit in the pan with the edges draping in another direction. Continue to fill the pan with 8 more phyllo sheets, brushing each sheet with butter.

3. Spoon the filling inside the pie and spread evenly.

4. Brush the remaining 6 sheets of phyllo one at a time and lay them on top. Turn up all the edges over the pie. It should look rough and crackly. Brush any remaining butter over the top.

5. Bake 1¼ hours, until the phyllo is golden brown and the filling is warmed through. Transfer to wire rack to cool. Carefully release the sides of the pan. Cut into wedges with a serrated knife.

TIP

Phyllo pastry is delicate and dries out quickly. Once you open the package and unroll the pastry sheets, keep them covered with a damp dishcloth while working.

Baked Potato Casserole

The beloved flavor combination of potatoes, milk, butter and chives come together here in a delicious easy-to-serve casserole.

1. Preheat oven to 400°F. Set oven rack to middle position.
2. Melt butter in a large saucepan or Dutch oven over medium heat until foaming. Add onion; cook 5 minutes, until softened, stirring often. Add thyme, salt and pepper; cook until fragrant, about 30 seconds. Add sliced potatoes, broth, milk and bay leaves; bring to a simmer. Cover, reduce heat to medium-low and simmer 10 minutes, until potatoes are almost tender. Discard bay leaves.
3. Transfer mixture to a buttered 2-quart casserole or 8-inch-square baking dish; sprinkle with cheese. Bake until casserole is bubbling around edges and top is golden brown, about 15 minutes. Cool 10 minutes, then sprinkle with chives before serving.

Serves 6

2 tablespoons unsalted butter, plus extra for pan

1 medium onion

1 teaspoon dried whole thyme

Salt and pepper, to taste

2½ pounds russet potatoes, peeled and thinly sliced

1 cup reduced-sodium chicken broth

1 cup whole milk

2 bay leaves

1½ cups coarsely grated Gruyère or Swiss cheese (about 6 ounces)

2 tablespoons minced chives, for garnish

Don't count on any leftovers with these potatoes, especially if Seth Gunderson is around.

TIP

You want the potatoes to be sliced very thinly. Keep them from sticking to the knife by adding a little cooking spray to the blade before slicing.

Baby Arugula Salad with Goat Cheese, Pecans and Pomegranate Seeds

Serves 8

1 small shallot, minced

3 tablespoons balsamic vinegar

1 teaspoon Dijon mustard

Salt and pepper, to taste

½ cup extra-virgin olive oil

10 to 12 cups baby arugula (about 10 ounces)

1 cup pomegranate seeds (from 1 pomegranate)

½ cup toasted pecans, chopped

1 cup crumbled goat cheese

TIP

Extra-virgin olive oil, which comes from the first cold pressing of the olives, has a stronger, purer flavor than virgin olive oil. Since it is more expensive, most cooks prefer to use it only for salad and other uncooked dishes. Virgin olive oil is better for sautéing.

This salad is a lively blend of sharp arugula, tangy goat cheese, mellow pecans and tart pomegranates. If you can't find arugula, substitute any delicate salad green.

1. In a glass measuring cup, whisk shallot, vinegar, mustard, salt and pepper until combined. Slowly pour oil in a stream until blended.
2. In a large serving bowl, combine arugula, pomegranate seeds and pecans. Add dressing; toss to coat. Top salad with cheese; toss once.

A perfect Christmas salad: Red and Green. It could almost be used as a table decoration. At least that's what Emily says.

Homemade Dinner Rolls

Makes 18

1¼-ounce package active dry yeast

1 cup water, divided

¼ cup granulated sugar, divided

1½ cups buttermilk

6 tablespoons unsalted butter, melted, plus extra for brushing

2 large eggs, lightly beaten

5 cups all-purpose flour

1 teaspoon baking soda

1¼ teaspoons salt

TIP

To test whether the dough has risen sufficiently, poke your finger in the dough; the impression should remain.

Light and fluffy, these yeasty dinner rolls get an extra rise from the addition of buttermilk and baking soda. They have a beautiful golden finish from a liberal brushing of butter just before they go in the oven.

1. In a small bowl, combine yeast with ¼ cup warm water and 1 tablespoon of the sugar. Stir and let stand 5 minutes. Yeast should be creamy and bubbling slightly.
2. In a 1-quart glass measuring cup, heat buttermilk in microwave until just warm. Stir in yeast mixture, melted butter, eggs and remaining sugar until combined.
3. In a large bowl, combine flour, baking soda and salt. Make a well in the center and pour in the buttermilk mixture. Fold with a spatula to form a craggy dough. Turn dough out onto a lightly floured surface and knead 6 minutes, until dough is smooth and elastic.
4. Lightly butter a large bowl. Place dough in bowl; turn to coat dough with butter. Cover bowl with plastic wrap and let stand in a warm, draft-free spot for 1½ hours, or until doubled.
5. Line a baking sheet with parchment paper. Punch down dough; knead quickly in bowl. Turn dough out onto a lightly floured work surface; cut into 18 pieces. Using your palm and fingers, roll each piece into a ball, tucking the dough underneath itself as you roll to form a taut ball. Repeat with remaining pieces. Transfer balls to prepared pan; cover with plastic wrap and let stand in a warm spot for 40 minutes, until almost doubled in size.
6. Preheat oven to 400°F. Brush tops of rolls with melted butter and bake 20 minutes, until golden brown.

Sautéed Green Beans and Almonds

The classic green bean and almond side dish is updated, allowing the fresh flavors to shine through without the gloppy cream sauce.

1. Warm oil in large nonstick skillet over medium heat until hot. Add beans, salt and pepper. Cook 6 minutes, shaking the pan often, until beans are brown in spots. Add ½ cup water; cover pot and cook 2 minutes, until beans are bright green but still crisp. Uncover; cook 1 minute, until water evaporates.
2. Add butter, garlic and tarragon; cook 2 minutes, until beans are tender-crisp and coated with butter. Transfer to serving bowl; sprinkle with almonds.

Serves 8

2 teaspoons olive oil

2 pounds green beans, trimmed and cut into 2-inch pieces

Salt and pepper, to taste

½ cup water

2 tablespoons unsalted butter

1 clove garlic, minced

2 teaspoons fresh tarragon, chopped

½ cup toasted slivered almonds

> **TIP**
>
> To toast almonds, cook them in an ungreased skillet over medium heat, stirring often, until golden.

Shirley Bliss told me her daughter once tried to hide the green beans under the tablecloth. The lumps gave her away.

Christmas Beef Wellington

Serves 10

1 tablespoon olive oil

1 beef tenderloin
(3 to 3½ pounds), tied

Salt and pepper, to taste

2 tablespoons unsalted butter

1 medium onion, chopped

1 pound white mushrooms,
stemmed and finely chopped

½ cup dry sherry or red wine

½ cup chopped fresh parsley

1 pound (2 sheets) frozen puff
pastry, thawed

¼ pound mushroom pâté

1 egg, lightly beaten

Kosher or sea salt,
for sprinkling

TIP

To save time, sear the beef
and cook the mushrooms the
day before. Both should be
stored in the refrigerator.

Beef tenderloin is one of the most tender and expensive cuts of beef. Ask your butcher to tie the tenderloin in 1-inch increments. If you can't find mushroom pâté in your grocery store, just leave it out—the recipe is delicious even without it.

1. Warm oil in large ovenproof skillet over medium-high heat. Season beef with salt and pepper. Brown on all sides, about 10 minutes total. Remove from heat; let rest until cool. Refrigerate until cold, about 1 hour.

2. Melt butter in large skillet over medium heat. Add onion, salt and pepper; cook 5 minutes, until softened, stirring often. Add mushrooms; cook 10 minutes, until liquid is released and cooked off, stirring often. Add sherry or red wine and cook 4 minutes, until mixture is dry. Remove from heat; season with salt and pepper, stir in parsley and let cool completely.

3. Lay both sheets of puff pastry end to end on a lightly floured countertop. Pinch the two ends together to seal and roll out pastry to form one 12-by-20-inch rectangle.

4. Spread half of the mushrooms over the puff pastry, leaving a 1-inch edge on all sides. Place the tenderloin in the center of the rectangle. Spread pâté over top and sides of tenderloin. Spread remaining sautéed mushrooms over the pâté. Brush the edges of the pastry with beaten egg, then fold the long edges over the tenderloin, pressing lightly to seal. Fold up and seal short ends of pasty. Use any excess dough to decorate the top as you like. Transfer meat, seam-side down, to baking sheet. Refrigerate 2 hours, or overnight.

5. Preheat oven to 400°F. Place another baking sheet on the middle rack in the oven until hot, about 15 minutes. Brush entire roast with remainder of beaten egg. Make 2 to 3 slits in pastry. Sprinkle with sea salt. Carefully transfer roast to preheated baking sheet.

6. Bake for 30 minutes. Reduce heat to 350°F. Bake 10 minutes longer, or until thermometer registers 130°F for medium-rare, and the pastry is cooked through. Let rest on a cutting board 10 minutes before slicing.

Jack Griffin's Christmas Cookies

Chocolate chips

Ritz crackers

Peanut butter

Holiday candy sprinkles or other small candies

TIP

Vary the candies in accordance with the holiday. Try holiday sprinkles at Christmas or Reese's Pieces at Halloween.

There are no exact amounts in this recipe. Just get a jar of peanut butter, a box of crackers, a bag of chocolate chips and the candies of your choice—and start creating!

1. Place a wire rack over a large sheet of wax or parchment paper.
2. Pour at least 1 cup chocolate chips in a glass bowl. Microwave in 1-minute increments until melted, stirring after each minute.
3. Spread peanut butter between 2 crackers to make a sandwich. (Refrain from eating it.) Dip sandwich in melted chocolate (or spread chocolate on sandwich) and place on wire rack. While still warm, sprinkle with candy. Store in refrigerator.

Only Jack could come up with something this clever, fun and delicious.

Shown on page 230

Holiday Sugar Cookies

This foolproof sugar cookie recipe makes a sturdy, sweet treat that's a perfect gift or a great addition to a holiday cookie platter.

1. In a large bowl with electric mixer on medium speed, cream butter and sugar until light and fluffy. Add eggs and vanilla; beat until combined.

2. In a separate bowl, combine flour, baking powder and salt. Reduce mixer speed to low; beat in flour mixture just until combined. Shape dough into two disks; wrap and refrigerate at least 2 hours or up to overnight.

3. Preheat oven to 350°F. Line baking sheets with parchment paper. Remove 1 dough disk from the refrigerator. Cut disk in half; cover remaining half. On a lightly floured surface with floured rolling pin, roll dough ¼-inch thick. Using cookie cutters, cut dough into as many cookies as possible; reserve trimmings for rerolling.

4. Place cookies on prepared sheets about 1 inch apart. Bake 10 to 12 minutes (depending on size of cookies) until pale gold. Transfer to wire rack to cool. Repeat with remaining dough and rerolled scraps.

Makes about 48 cookies

2 cups (4 sticks) unsalted butter, at room temperature

2 cups brown sugar

2 large eggs

2 teaspoons vanilla extract or grated lemon peel

6 cups all-purpose flour, plus extra for rolling

2 teaspoons baking powder

1 teaspoon salt

TIP

Decorate baked cookies with prepared frosting or sprinkle unbaked cookies with colored sugars before putting them in the oven.

Shown on page 230

Gingerbread Men

If desired, press raisins, chocolate chips or red-hot candies into dough for eyes and buttons before baking. Store in airtight container with a sheet of waxed or parchment paper between each layer.

1. In a medium heavy saucepan over medium heat, bring molasses, brown sugar, all of the spices and salt to a simmer. Remove from heat; stir in baking soda (mixture will bubble). Drop in butter pieces one at a time, stirring constantly so the butter melts. Pour into a large mixing bowl. Stir in beaten egg. Fold in flour.

2. Knead dough in bowl for 1 minute, adding a little more flour if needed to prevent sticking. Divide into 2 disks; wrap each in plastic. Refrigerate at least 1 hour and up to 2 days.

3. Preheat oven to 325°F. On a lightly floured countertop, roll to a 14-inch round, about ¼-inch thick. Cut out as many cookies as possible and transfer to prepared sheets. Repeat with remaining dough and rerolled scraps.

4. Bake 10 to 12 minutes, until cookies are set in center and edges are slightly browned. Halfway through baking, rotate cookie sheets front to back and switch positions top to bottom. Do not overbake. Remove with spatula to wire rack to cool completely.

Makes about 48 cookies

⅔ cup molasses

⅔ cup dark brown sugar

1 tablespoon ground cinnamon

1 tablespoon ground ginger

½ teaspoon ground cloves

¼ teaspoon ground allspice

½ teaspoon salt

2 teaspoons baking soda

1 cup (2 sticks) unsalted butter, cut into chunks

1 large egg, lightly beaten

4 cups all-purpose flour, plus extra for rolling

TIP

For thin and crispy cookies, roll to ⅛-inch thickness and bake for 16 to 18 minutes.

Acknowledgments

My best ideas usually come from readers, and this book is a prime example. From the moment I mentioned Peggy Beldon's homemade blueberry muffins in *44 Cranberry Point*, I started getting reader requests for the recipe. It wasn't long before other readers suggested it would be a "good idea" to publish a Cedar Cove cookbook. I took this good idea to my publisher. It then went to Deborah Brody, Executive Editor for Nonfiction, who gave the project an enthusiastic go-ahead.

Deborah, who is as charming as she is smart, brought Susie Ott on board. Susie, a recipe developer, scrutinized all the recipes and tested each and every one. She told me several were a big hit with her doorman, who was more than willing to give them the taste test, along with her husband and family.

I hope you're as excited about this lovely book as I am. Susi Oberhelman is the talented designer who worked on these pages. Andy Ryan is the very skilled food photographer. (Don't the dishes look wonderful?) And food stylist Catrine Kelty and prop stylist Sylvia Lacher made each one as appealing to the eye as to the taste buds.

The photo of me in my kitchen was taken by Nina Subin. She promised to make me look thin—but who'd trust a thin cook? That was a photo shoot I'll long remember. I had three women rummaging through my closet looking for just the right outfit. (I wonder if Christie Brinkley's clothes go through that kind of scrutiny?) Thankfully, all three are so talented and such fun that I had hardly a word of complaint, although I did argue about the peach-colored sweater. My three stylists, in case anyone disagrees with their choice of outfit, are Margie Miller, Amy Jones and Tara Kelly. I can't remember laughing that hard in a long time.

No acknowledgment page would be complete without mention of my wonderful editor, Paula Eykelhof. Paula and I have worked together going on twenty-four years now. We like to think of ourselves as Helen Keller and Annie Sullivan, although we often reverse roles. We've grown up in the business together and make a great team.

Special thanks to my agent, Theresa Park, who is wise beyond her years and has blessed me and my career in many ways.

And last, but certainly not least, thanks to my husband, Wayne, who volunteered to fly to New York and taste test each recipe along with Susie Ott's doorman. I love you, Wayne. The next time you ask, "What's for dinner?" I'll have an answer.

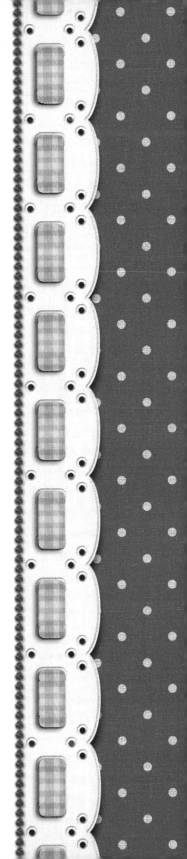

CONVERSION CHART

WEIGHT

1 ounce	28 g
4 ounces *or* ¼ pound	113 g
⅓ pound	150 g
8 ounces *or* ½ pound	230 g
⅔ pound	300 g
12 ounces *or* ¾ pound	340 g
1 pound *or* 16 ounces	450 g
2 pounds	900 g
2.2 pounds	1 kilogram

TEMPERATURES

Fahrenheit	Celsius
212 °	100°
250°	120°
275 °	140°
300°	150°
325°	160°
350°	180°
375°	190°
400°	200°
425°	220°
450°	230°
475°	240°
500°	260°

VOLUME

1 teaspoon	5 ml
1 tablespoon *or* ½ fluid ounce	15 ml
1 fluid ounce *or* ⅛ cup	30 ml
¼ *or* 2 fluid ounces	60 ml
⅓ cup	80 ml
½ cup *or* 4 fluid ounces	120 ml
⅔ cup	160 ml
¾ cup *or* 6 fluid ounces	180 ml
1 cup *or* 8 fluid ounces *or* half a pint	240 ml
1½ cups *or* 12 fluid ounces	350 ml
2 cups *or* 1 pint *or* 16 fluid ounces	475 ml
3 cups *or* 1½ pints	700 ml
4 cups *or* 2 pints *or* 1 quart	950 ml
4 quarts *or* 1 gallon	3.8 liters

Index

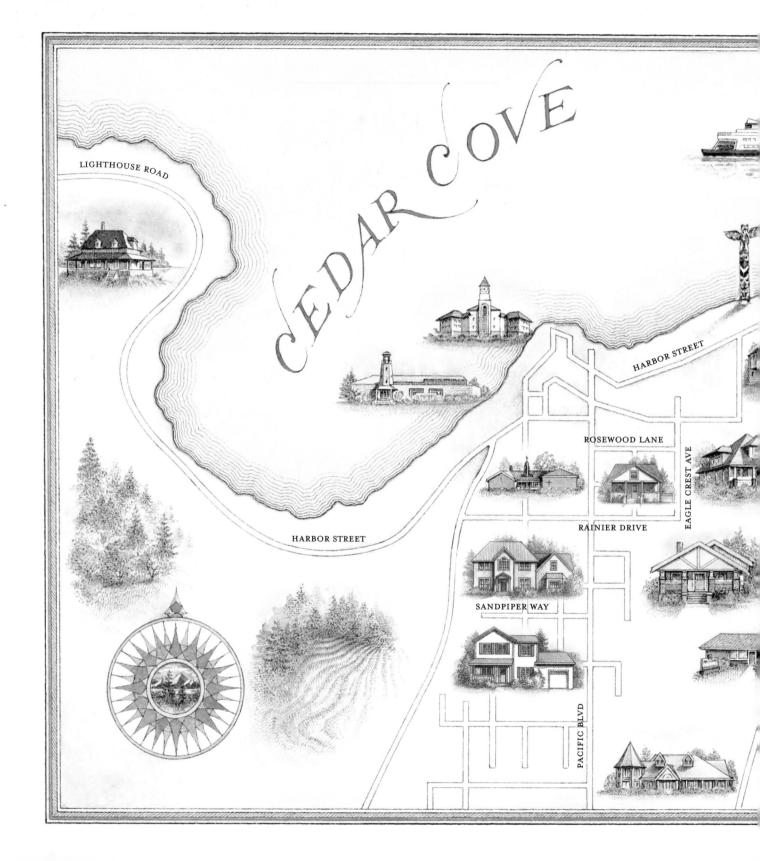

CEDAR COVE

LIGHTHOUSE ROAD

HARBOR STREET

HARBOR STREET

ROSEWOOD LANE

EAGLE CREST AVE

RAINIER DRIVE

SANDPIPER WAY

PACIFIC BLVD